Poems
that will
save
your
Life

Poems

that will

save

your

Life

Edited by John Boyes

ARCTURUS

ARCTURUS

This edition published in 2014 by Arcturus Publishing Limited
26/27 Bickels Yard, 151–153 Bermondsey Street,
London SE1 3HA

ISBN: 978-1-84837-574-1
AD001375NT

Printed in China

Contents

Introduction

There are poems in this collection that were written by unknown hands. While they may lack the talent and artfulness of the great poets in the English language, their voices are just as legitimate. And so, their work is presented here beside that of names like John Keats, Christina Rossetti, Walt Whitman and Emily Dickinson.

It may be argued that these anonymous poems are the most beloved. These are, after all, lines that have been handed down through the generations. Where heavy volumes of verse by Robert Browning and Henry Wadsworth Longfellow may have been presented as graduation and Christmas gifts, these less recognized poems have countless times been lovingly transcribed and passed on as having particularly pertinent messages. These are words of encouragement and comfort, written perhaps in reaction, perhaps in anticipation.

We cannot know what motivation and inspiration brought these anonymously penned poems into being. Of much of the other verse, that written by known figures, including the acclaimed and celebrated, we may still only speculate. There are, however, some poems for which the respective seeds are known. 'Song of Myself', which first saw print in 1856 as 'Poem of Walt Whitman, an American', was written in part to encourage national unity in the years immediately preceding the advent of civil war in the United States.

Related to this, we find John Greenleaf Whittier's 'Laus Deo!', written, as the poet says, 'on hearing the bells ring on the passage of the constitutional amendment abolishing slavery'. Reading this poem, nearly fifteen decades after its composition, one shares in the joy felt by a man who had devoted his life to the Abolitionist cause, a man whose strong Quaker faith abhorred what he saw as the sin of slavery.

Whittier was entering old age when he saw his dream realized. Not all are so lucky. Various poems included in this volume are an address to those who have fallen short of their goals, those whose aspirations have been unfulfilled. It is not at all unusual for the disappointed and distressed to turn to poetry when seeking consolation. Indeed, the earliest verse featured in this anthology, the 23rd Psalm, is a poem of comfort. Found in the Hebrew Bible and the Old Testament, this verse is ascribed by tradition to David, who is thought to have reigned over the Kingdom of Israel roughly three thousand years ago. It holds a strong place in Judaism and has come to have a central presence in Christian funerals.

The 23rd Psalm is at once a poem of comfort and a poem of faith. This cannot be surprising in that people often seek comfort in faith. The finest poets in the English language have expressed their spirituality in verse. This includes such diverse voices as Gerard Manley Hopkins, a Jesuit priest, and D. H. Lawrence, who will be forever remembered as the writer of *Lady Chatterley's Lover*.

Lawrence wrote at a time when the self-help movement was in its infancy. Today, eight decades after his death, it has a significant presence in bookstores, conference centres, and on television. We have motivational speakers – celebrities in their own right – who receive good money for their words of inspiration and encouragement. And yet, their messages aren't new, nor is their advice. We see this very same wisdom expressed more eloquently by George Eliot, Henry David Thoreau, Alfred, Lord Tennyson . . . and, yes, Anonymous.

John Boyes

POEMS OF INSPIRATION

The Road Not Taken

Two roads diverged in a yellow wood,
And sorry I could not travel both
And be one traveler, long I stood
And looked down one as far as I could
To where it bent in the undergrowth;

Then took the other, as just as fair,
And having perhaps the better claim,
Because it was grassy and wanted wear;
Though as for that the passing there
Had worn them really about the same,

And both that morning equally lay
In leaves no step had trodden black.
Oh, I kept the first for another day!
Yet knowing how way leads on to way,
I doubted if I should ever come back.

I shall be telling this with a sigh
Somewhere ages and ages hence:
Two roads diverged in a wood, and I—
I took the one less traveled by,
And that has made all the difference.

— *Robert Frost*

If I Can Stop One Heart From Breaking

If I can stop one heart from breaking,
I shall not live in vain;
If I can ease one life the aching,
Or cool one pain,
Or help one fainting robin
Unto his nest again,
I shall not live in vain.

— *Emily Dickinson*

The Inner Vision

Most sweet it is with unuplifted eyes
    To pace the ground, if path there be or none,
While a fair region round the traveller lies
    Which he forbears again to look upon;
Pleased rather with some soft ideal scene,
    The work of Fancy, or some happy tone
Of meditation, slipping in between
    The beauty coming and the beauty gone.
—If Thought and Love desert us, from that day
    Let us break off all commerce with the Muse:
With Thought and Love companions of our way—
    Whate'er the senses take or may refuse,—
    The Mind's internal heaven shall shed her dews
Of inspiration on the humblest lay.

— *William Wordsworth*

Inspiration

Whate'er we leave to God, God does,
    And blesses us;
The work we choose should be our own,
    God leaves alone.

If with light head erect I sing,
    Though all the Muses lend their force,
From my poor love of anything,
    The verse is weak and shallow as its source.

But if with bended neck I grope,
    Listening behind me for my wit,
With faith superior to hope,
    More anxious to keep back than forward it,

Making my soul accomplice there
    Unto the flame my heart hath lit,
Then will the verse forever wear—
    Time cannot bend the line which God hath
        writ.

Always the general show of things
    Floats in review before my mind,
And such true love and reverence brings,
    That sometimes I forget that I am blind.

But now there comes unsought, unseen,
    Some clear divine electuary,
And I, who had but sensual been,
    Grow sensible, and as God is, am wary.

I hearing get, who had but ears,
    And sight, who had but eyes before,
I moments live, who lived but years,
    And truth discern, who knew but learning's
        lore.

I hear beyond the range of sound,
    I see beyond the range of sight,
New earths and skies and seas around,
    And in my day the sun doth pale his light.

A clear and ancient harmony
    Pierces my soul through all its din,
As through its utmost melody—
    Farther behind than they—farther within.

More swift its bolt than lightning is,
    Its voice than thunder is more loud,
It doth expand my privacies
    To all, and leave me single in the crowd.

It speaks with such authority,
    With so serene and lofty tone,
That idle Time runs gadding by,
    And leaves me with Eternity alone.

Then chiefly is my natal hour,
    And only now my prime of life,
Of manhood's strength it is the flower,
    'Tis peace's end and war's beginning strife.

'T hath come in summer's broadest noon,
    By a gray wall or some chance place,
Unseasoning time, insulting June,
    And vexing day with its presuming face.

Such fragrance round my couch it makes,
    More rich than are Arabian drugs,
That my soul scents its life and wakes
    The body up beneath its perfumed rugs.

Such is the Muse—the heavenly maid,
    The star that guides our mortal course,
Which shows where life's true kernel's laid,
    Its wheat's fine flour, and its undying force.

She with one breath attunes the spheres,
    And also my poor human heart,
With one impulse propels the years
    Around, and gives my throbbing pulse its
        start.

I will not doubt for evermore,
    Nor falter from a steadfast faith,
For thought the system be turned o'er,
    God takes not back the word which once He
    saith.

I will then trust the love untold
    Which not my worth nor want has bought,
Which wooed me young, and woos me old,
    And to this evening hath me brought.

My memory I'll educate
  To know the one historic truth,
Remembering to the latest date
  The only true and sole immortal youth.

Be but thy inspiration given,
  No matter through what danger sought,
I'll fathom hell or climb to heaven,
  And yet esteem that cheap which love has
    bought.

Fame cannot tempt the bard
  Who's famous with his God,
Nor laurel him reward
  Who has his Maker's nod.

— *Henry David Thoreau*

The Common Problem

from *Bishop Blougram's Apology*

The common problem, yours, mine, every one's,
Is—not to fancy what were fair in life
Provided it could be,—but, finding first
What may be, then find how to make it fair
Up to our means: a very different thing!

— *Robert Browning*

A Psalm to Life

Tell me not, in mournful numbers,
    Life is but an empty dream!—
For the soul is dead that slumbers,
    And things are not what they seem.

Life is real! Life is earnest!
    And the grave is not its goal;
Dust thou art, to dust returnest,
    Was not spoken of the soul.

Not enjoyment, and not sorrow,
    Is our destined end or way;
But to act, that each to-morrow
    Find us farther than to-day.

Art is long, and Time is fleeting,
    And our hearts, though stout and brave,
Still, like muffled drums, are beating
    Funeral marches to the grave.

In the world's broad field of battle,
    In the bivouac of Life,
Be not like dumb, driven cattle!
    Be a hero in the strife!

Trust no Future, howe'er pleasant!
    Let the dead Past bury its dead!
Act,—act in the living Present!
    Heart within, and God o'erhead!

Lives of great men all remind us
    We can make our lives sublime,
And, departing, leave behind us
    Footprints on the sands of time;

Footprints, that perhaps another,
    Sailing o'er life's solemn main,
A forlorn and shipwrecked brother,
    Seeing, shall take heart again.

Let us, then, be up and doing,
    With a heart for any fate;
Still achieving, still pursuing,
    Learn to labor and to wait.

— *Henry Wadsworth Longfellow*

Drop a Pebble in the Water

Drop a pebble in the water: just a splash, and it
is gone;
But there's half-a-hundred ripples circling on
and on and on,
Spreading, spreading from the center, flowing on
out to the sea.
And there is no way of telling where the end
is going to be.

Drop a pebble in the water: in a minute you
forget,
But there's little waves a-flowing, and there's
ripples circling yet,
And those little waves a-flowing to a great big
wave have grown;
You've disturbed a mighty river just by
dropping in a stone.

Drop an unkind word, or careless: in a minute it
is gone;
But there's half-a-hundred ripples circling on
and on and on.
They keep spreading, spreading, spreading from
the center as they go,
And there is no way to stop them, once
you've started them to flow.

Drop an unkind word, or careless: in a minute
you forget;
But there's little waves a-flowing, and there's
ripples circling yet,
And perhaps in some sad heart a mighty wave of
tears you've stirred,
And disturbed a life was happy ere you
dropped that unkind word.

Drop a word of cheer and kindness: just a flash
and it is gone;
But there's half-a-hundred ripples circling on
and on and on,
Bearing hope and joy and comfort on each
splashing, dashing wave
Till you wouldn't believe the volume of the
one kind word you gave.

Drop a word of cheer and kindness: in a minute
  you forget;
    But there's gladness still a-swelling, and
      there's joy a-circling yet,
And you've rolled a wave of comfort whose
  sweet music can be heard
    Over miles and miles of water just by
      dropping one kind word.

— *James W. Foley*

Today I...

Today I smiled, and all at once things didn't look
so bad.
Today I shared with someone else, a bit of
hope I had.
Today I sang a little song, and felt my heart grow
light,
And walked a happy little mile, with not a
cloud in sight.

Today I worked with what I had and longed for
nothing more,
And what had seemed like only weeds, were
flowers at my door.
Today I loved a little more and complained a
little less,
And in the giving of myself, I forgot my
weariness.

— *Anonymous*

Contentment

I weigh not fortune's frown or smile:
    I joy not much in earthly joys:
I seek not state, I reck not style;
    I am not fond of fancy's toys;
I rest so pleased with what I have
I wish no more, no more I crave.

I quake not at the thunder's crack;
    I tremble not at news of war;
I swound not at the news of wrack;
    I shrink not at a blazing star;
I fear no loss, I hope not gain,
I envy none, I none disdain.

I see ambition, never pleased;
    I see some Tantals starved in store;
I see gold's dropsy seldom eased;
    I see even Midas gape for more;
I neither want nor yet abound,—
    Enough's a feast, content is crowned.

I feign not friendship where I hate;
    I fawn not on the great (in show);
I prize, I praise a mean estate,—
    Neither too lofty nor too low:
This, this is all my choice, my cheer,—
A mind content, a conscience clear.

— *Joshua Sylvester*

The Builders

All are architects of Fate,
    Working in these walls of Time;
Some with massive deeds and great,
    Some with ornaments of rhyme.
Nothing useless is, or low;
    Each thing in its place is best;
And what seems but idle show
    Strengthens and supports the rest.
For the structure that we raise,
    Time is with materials filled;
Our to-days and yesterdays
    Are the blocks with which we build.
Truly shape and fashion these;
    Leave no yawning gaps between;
Think not, because no man sees,
    Such things will remain unseen.
In the elder days of Art,
    Builders wrought with greatest care
Each minute and unseen part;
    For the Gods see everywhere.
Let us do our work as well,
    Both the unseen and the seen;

Make the house, where Gods may dwell,
    Beautiful, entire, and clean.
Else our lives are incomplete,
    Standing in these walls of Time,
Broken stairways, where the feet
    Stumble as they seek to climb.
Build to-day, then, strong and sure,
    With a firm and ample base;
And ascending and secure
    Shall to-morrow find its place.
Thus alone can we attain
    To those turrets, where the eye
Sees the world as one vast plain,
    And one boundless reach of sky.

— *Henry Wadsworth Longfellow*

Giving Your Best

It's the hand we clasp with an honest grasp
That gives a hearty thrill;
It's the good we pour into others' lives
That comes back our own to fill.
It's the dregs we drain from another's cup
That makes our own seem sweet;
And the hours we give to another's need
That makes our life complete.
It's the burdens we help another bear
That makes our own seem light.
It's the anger seen for another's feet
That shows us the path to right.
It's the good we do each passing day,
With a heart sincere and true;
In giving the world your very best
Its best will return to you.

— *Anonymous*

Nobility

True worth is in *being*, not *seeming*,—
    In doing, each day that goes by,
Some little good—not in dreaming
    Of great things to do by and by.
For whatever men say in their blindness,
    And spite of the fancies of youth,
There's nothing so kingly as kindness,
    And nothing so royal as truth. ·

We get back our mete as we measure—
    We cannot do wrong and feel right,
Nor can we give pain and gain pleasure,
    For justice avenges each slight.
The air for the wing of the sparrow,
    The bush for the robin and wren,
But always the path that is narrow
    And straight, for the children of men.

'Tis not in the pages of story
    The heart of its ills to beguile,
Though he who makes courtship to glory
    Gives all that he hath for her smile.

For when from her heights he has won her,
    Alas! it is only to prove
That nothing's so sacred as honor,
    And nothing so loyal as love!

We cannot make bargains for blisses,
    Nor catch them like fishes in nets;
And sometimes the thing our life misses
    Helps more than the thing which it gets.
For good lieth not in pursuing,
    Nor gaining of great nor of small,
But just in the doing, and doing
    As we would be done by, is all.

Through envy, through malice, through hating,
    Against the world, early and late,
No jot of our courage abating—
    Our part is to work and to wait.
And slight is the sting of his trouble
    Whose winnings are less than his worth;
For he who is honest is noble,
    Whatever his fortunes of birth.

— *Alice Cary*

For Beauty Being the Best of All We Know

For beauty being the best of all we know
Sums up the unsearchable and secret aims
Of nature, and on joys whose earthly names
Were never told can form and sense bestow;
And man has sped his instinct to outgo
The step of science; and against her shames
Imagination stakes out heavenly claims,
Building a tower above the head of woe.
Nor is there fairer work for beauty found
Than that she win in nature her release
From all the woes that in the world abound;
Nay with his sorrow may his love increase,
If from man's greater need beauty redound,
And claim his tears for homage of his peace.

— *Robert Bridges*

My Creed

To live as gently as I can;
To be, no matter where, a man;
To take what comes of good or ill
And cling to faith and honor still;
To do my best, and let that stand
The record of my brain and hand;
And then, should failure come to me,
Still work and hope for victory.

To have no secret place wherein
I stoop unseen to shame or sin;
To be the same when I'm alone
As when my every deed is known
To live undaunted, unafraid
Of any step that I have made;
To be without pretense or sham
Exactly what men think I am.

To leave some simple mark behind
To keep my having lived in mind,
If enmity to aught I show,
To be an honest, generous foe,
To play my little part, nor whine
That greater honors are not mine.
This, I believe, is all I need
For my philosophy and creed.

— *Edgar Guest*

POEMS OF ENCOURAGEMENT

The Sin of Omission

It isn't the thing you do, dear;
   It's the thing you leave undone,
That gives you a bit of a heartache
   At the setting of the sun.
The tender word forgotten,
   The letter you did not write,
The flowers you did not send, dear,
   Are your haunting ghosts to-night.

The stone you might have lifted
   Out of a brother's way,
The bit of heartsome counsel
   You were hurried too much to say;
The loving touch of the hand, dear,
   The gentle and winsome tone,
Which you had no time nor thought for,
   With troubles enough of your own.

Those little acts of kindness
   So easily out of mind;
Those chances to be angels
   Which we poor mortals find—

They come in night and silence—
    Each sad, reproachful wraith—
When hope is faint and flagging,
    And a chill has fallen on faith.

For life is all too short, dear,
    And sorrow is all too great;
To suffer our slow compassion
    That tarries until too late;
And it isn't the thing you do, dear,
    It's the thing you leave undone,
Which gives you a bit of a heartache
    At the setting of the sun.

— *Margaret E. Sangster*

Forbearance

Hast thou named all the birds without a gun?
Loved the wood-rose, and left it on its stalk?
At rich men's tables eaten bread and pulse?
Unarmed, faced danger with a heart of trust?
And loved so well a high behavior,
In man or maid, that thou from speech refrained,
Nobility more nobly to repay?
O, be my friend, and teach me to be thine!

— *Ralph Waldo Emerson*

Tell All the Truth but Tell it Slant—

Tell all the Truth but tell it slant—
Success in Circuit lies
Too bright for our infirm Delight
The Truth's superb surprise

As Lightning to the Children eased
With explanation kind
The Truth must dazzle gradually
Or every man be blind—

— *Emily Dickinson*

The Means to Attain Happy Life

Martial, the things that do attain
    The happy life be these, I find:—
The richesse left, not got with pain;
    The fruitful ground, the quiet mind;

The equal friend; no grudge, no strife;
    No charge of rule, nor governance;
Without disease, the healthful life;
    The household of continuance;

The mean diet, no delicate fare;
    True wisdom join'd with simpleness;
The night dischargèd of all care,
    Where wine the wit may not oppress.

The faithful wife, without debate;
    Such sleeps as may beguile the night:
Contented with thine own estate
    Ne wish for death, ne fear his might.

— *Henry Howard*

Grammar

Live in the active voice, rather than passive.
Think more about what you happen than what is
happening to you.

Live in the indicative mood, rather than in the
subjunctive.
Be concerned with things as they are, rather than
as they might be

Live in the present tense, facing the duty at hand
without regret for the past or worry over the
future.

Live in the singular number, caring more for the
approval of your own conscience
than for the applause of the crowd.

— *William De Witt Hyde*

The Character of a Happy Life

How happy is he born and taught
That serveth not another's will;
Whose armour is his honest thought,
And simple truth his utmost skill!

Whose passions not his masters are;
Whose soul is still prepared for death,
Untied unto the world by care
Of public fame or private breath;

Who envies none that chance doth raise,
Nor vice; who never understood
How deepest wounds are given by praise;
Nor rules of state, but rules of good;

Who hath his life from rumours freed;
Whose conscience is his strong retreat;
Whose state can neither flatterers feed,
Nor ruin make oppressors great;

Who God doth late and early pray
More of His grace than gifts to lend;
And entertains the harmless day
With a religious book or friend;

—This man is freed from servile bands
Of hope to rise or fear to fall:
Lord of himself, though not of lands,
And having nothing, yet hath all.

— *Sir Henry Wotton*

Why Thus Longing?

Why thus longing, thus forever sighing,
　For the far-off, unattained, and dim,
While the beautiful, all round thee lying,
　Offers up its low, perpetual hymn?

Wouldst thou listen to its gentle teaching,
　All thy restless yearnings it would still;
Leaf and flower and laden bee are preaching
　Thine own sphere, though humble, first to fill.

Poor indeed thou must be, if around thee
　Thou no ray of light and joy canst throw—
If no silken cord of love hath bound thee
　To some little world through weal and woe;

If no dear eyes thy fond love can brighten—
　No fond voices answer to thine own;
If no brother's sorrow thou canst lighten,
　By daily sympathy and gentle tone.

Not by deeds that win the crowd's applauses,
    Not by works that give thee world-renown,
Not by martyrdom or vaunted crosses,
    Canst thou win and wear the immortal crown!

Daily struggling, though unloved and lonely,
    Every day a rich reward will give;
Thou wilt find, by hearty striving only,
    And truly loving, thou canst truly live.

Dost thou revel in the rosy morning,
    When all nature hails the lord of light,
And his smile, the mountain-tops adorning,
    Robes yon fragrant fields in radiance bright?

Other hands may grasp the field and forest,
    Proud proprietors in pomp may shine;
But with fervent love if thou adorest,
    Thou art wealthier—all the world is thine.

Yet if through earth's wide domains thou rovest,
    Sighing that they are not thine alone,
Not those fair fields, but thyself, thou lovest,
    And their beauty and thy wealth are gone.

Nature wears the color of the spirit;
    Sweetly to her worshipper she sings;
All the glow, the grace she doth inherit,
    Round her trusting child she fondly flings.

— *Harriet Winslow Sewall*

We Scatter Seeds

We scatter seeds with careless hand,
    And dream we ne'er shall see them more;
        But for a thousand years
        Their fruit appears,
In weeds that mar the land,
    Or healthful store.

The deeds we do, the words we say,—
    Into still air they seem to fleet,
        We count them ever past;
        But they shall last,—
In the dread judgment they
    And we shall meet.

I charge thee by the years gone by,
    For the love's sake of brethren dear,
        Keep thou the one true way,
        In work and play,
Lest in that world their cry
    Of woe thou hear.

— *John Keble*

Destiny

Somewhere there waiteth in this world of ours
For one lone soul another lonely soul
Each choosing each through all the weary hours
And meeting strangely at one sudden goal.
Then blend they, like green leaves with golden
    flowers
Into one beautiful and perfect whole;
And life's long night is ended, and the way
Lies open onward to eternal day.

— *Sir Edwin Arnold*

Thanatopsis

To him who in the love of Nature holds
Communion with her visible forms, she speaks
A various language; for his gayer hours
She has a voice of gladness, and a smile
And eloquence of beauty, and she glides
Into his darker musings, with a mild
And healing sympathy, that steals away
Their sharpness, ere he is aware. When thoughts
Of the last bitter hour come like a blight
Over thy spirit, and sad images
Of the stern agony, and shroud, and pall,
And breathless darkness, and the narrow house,
Make thee to shudder, and grow sick at heart;—
Go forth under the open sky, and list
To Nature's teachings, while from all around—
Earth and her waters, and the depths of air—
Comes a still voice—Yet a few days, and thee
The all-beholding sun shall see no more
In all his course; nor yet in the cold ground,
Where thy pale form was laid, with many tears,
Nor in the embrace of ocean, shall exist
Thy image. Earth, that nourished thee, shall claim

Thy growth, to be resolved to earth again,
And, lost each human trace, surrendering up
Thine individual being, shalt thou go
To mix forever with the elements;
To be a brother to the insensible rock,
And to the sluggish clod, which the rude swain
Turns with his share, and treads upon. The oak
Shall send his roots abroad, and pierce thy
  mould.
  Yet not to thine eternal resting-place
Shalt thou retire alone, nor couldst thou wish
Couch more magnificent. Thou shalt lie down

With patriarchs of the infant world,—with kings,
The powerful of the earth,—the wise, the good,
Fair forms, and hoary seers of ages past,
All in one mighty sepulchre. The hills
Rock-ribbed and ancient as the sun; the vales
Stretching in pensive quietness between;
The venerable woods—rivers that move
In majesty, and the complaining brooks
That make the meadows green; and, poured
    round all,
Old Ocean's gray and melancholy waste,—
Are but the solemn decorations all

Of the great tomb of man! The golden sun,
The planets, all the infinite host of heaven,
Are shining on the sad abodes of death,
Through the still lapse of ages. All that tread
The globe are but a handful to the tribes
That slumber in its bosom.—Take the wings
Of morning, pierce the Barcan wilderness,
Or lose thyself in the continuous woods
Where rolls the Oregon, and hears no sound,
Save his own dashings,—yet the dead are there:
And millions in those solitudes, since first
The flight of years began, have laid them down
In their last sleep—the dead reign there alone.
So shalt thou rest; and what if thou withdraw
In silence from the living, and no friend
Take note of thy departure? All that breathe
Will share thy destiny. The gay will laugh
When thou art gone, the solemn brood of care
Plod on, and each one as before will chase
His favorite phantom; yet all these shall leave
Their mirth and their employments, and shall
    come

And make their bed with thee. As the long train
Of ages glide away, the sons of men,
The youth in life's green spring, and he who goes
In the full strength of years, matron and maid,
The speechless babe, and the gray-headed
    man—
Shall one by one be gathered to thy side
By those, who in their turn shall follow them.

So live, that when thy summons comes to join
The innumerable caravan which moves
To that mysterious realm, where each shall take
His chamber in the silent halls of death,
Thou go not, like the quarry-slave at night,
Scourged to his dungeon, but, sustained and
    soothed
By an unfaltering trust, approach thy grave
Like one who wraps the drapery of his couch
About him, and lies down to pleasant dreams.

— *William Cullen Bryant*

Remember

Remember me when I am gone away,
　　Gone far away into the silent land;
　　When you can no more hold me by the hand,
Nor I half turn to go, yet turning stay.
Remember me when no more day by day
　　You tell me of our future that you plann'd:
　　Only remember me; you understand
It will be late to counsel then or pray.
Yet if you should forget me for a while
　　And afterwards remember, do not grieve:
　　For if the darkness and corruption leave
A vestige of the thoughts that once I had,
Better by far you should forget and smile
　　Than that you should remember and be sad.

— *Christina Rossetti*

Life's Mirror

There are loyal hearts, there are spirits brave,
There are souls that are pure and true,
Then give to the world the best you have,
And the best will come back to you.

Give love, and love to your life will flow,
A strength in your utmost need,
Have faith, and a score of hearts will show
Their faith in your word and deed.

Give truth, and your gift will be paid in kind;
And honor will honor meet;
And a smile that is sweet will surely find
A smile that is just as sweet.

Give pity and sorrow to those who mourn,
You will gather in flowers again
The scattered seeds from your thoughts outborne
Though the sowing seemed but vain.

For life is the mirror of king and slave,
'Tis just what we are and do;
Then give to the world the best you have,
And the best will come back to you.

— *Madeline S. Bridges*

A Poem to Hope

Never go gloomy, use your mind,
Hope is a better companion than fear;

Providence, ever benignant and kind,
Gives with a smile what you take with a tear;

All will be right,
Look to the light.

Morning was ever the daughter of night;
All that was black will be all that is bright.

Many a foe is a friend in disguise,
Many a trouble a blessing most true,

Remember these words of wisdom and wise,
Your life will be easier and you will not be blue.

Never lose your hope, follow your plan
And live life doing all that you can.

— *Anonymous*

Thought

Thought is deeper than all speech,
    Feeling deeper than all thought:
Souls to souls can never teach
    What unto themselves was taught.

We are spirits clad in veils:
    Man by man was never seen:
All our deep communing fails
    To remove the shadowy screen.

Heart to heart was never known:
    Mind with mind did never meet:
We are columns left alone,
    Of a temple once complete.

Like the stars the gem the sky,
    Far apart, though seeming near,
In our light we scattered lie;
    All is thus but starlight here.

What is social company
  But a babbling summer stream?
What our wise philosophy
  But the glancing of a dream?

Only when the Sun of Love
  Melts the scattered stars of thought;
Only when we live above
  What the dim-eyed world hath taught,

Only when our souls are fed
  By the Fount which gave them birth,
And by inspiration led,
  Which they never drew from earth,

We, like parted drops of rain,
  Swelling till they meet and run,
Shall be all absorbed again,
  Melting, flowing into one.

— *Christopher Pearse Cranch*

The Tone of Voice

It's not so much what you say,
As the manner in which you say it;
It's not so much the language you use
As the tone in which you convey it;
'Come here!' I sharply said,
And the child cowered and wept.
'Come here', I said—
He looked and smiled
And straight to my lap he crept.
Words may be mild and fair
And the tone may pierce like a dart;
Words may be soft as the summer air,
But the tone may break my heart;
For words come from the mind
Grow by study and art—
But tone leaps from the inner self,
Revealing the state of heart.
Whether you know it or not,
Whether you mean or care,
Gentleness, kindness, love, and hate,
Envy, anger are there.
Then, would you quarrels avoid

And peace and love rejoice?
Keep anger not only out of your words—
Keep it out of your voice.

— *Anonymous*

A Friend

What is a Friend? I'll tell you.
It is a person with whom you dare to be yourself.
Your soul can go naked with him.
He seems to ask you to put on nothing, only to
be what you really are.
When you are with him, you do not have to be
on your guard.
You can say what you think, so long as it is
genuinely you.
He understands those contradictions in your
nature that cause others to misjudge you.
With him you breathe freely—you can avow
your little vanities and envies and absurdities
and in opening them up to him they are
dissolved on the white ocean of his loyalty.
He understands.—You can weep with him, laugh
with him, pray with him—through and
underneath it all he sees, knows and loves you.
A Friend, I repeat, is one with whom *you dare to
be yourself*.

— *Anonymous*

POEMS OF STRENGTH

Life's Lessons

After a while you learn the difference,
between holding a hand and chaining a soul.
You learn that love isn't leaning,
but lending support.
You begin to accept your defeats with the grace
    of an adult,
not the grief of a child.
You decide to build your roads on today,
for tomorrow's ground is too uncertain.
You help someone plant a garden,
instead of waiting for someone to bring you
    flowers.
You learn that God has given you the strength to
    endure,
and that you really do have worth.

— *Anonymous*

Prospice

Fear death?—to feel the fog in my throat,
    The mist in my face,
When the snows begin, and the blasts denote
    I am nearing the place,
The power of the night, the press of the storm,
    The post of the foe;
Where he stands, the Arch Fear in a visible
    form,
    Yet the strong man must go:
For the journey is done and the summit attained,
    And the barriers fall,
Though a battle's to fight ere the guerdon be
    gained,
    The reward of it all.
I was ever a fighter, so—one fight more,
    The best and the last!
I would hate that death bandaged my eyes, and
    forbore,
    And bade me creep past.
No! let me taste the whole of it, fare like my
    peers
    The heroes of old,

Bear the brunt, in a minute pay glad life's arrears
    Of pain, darkness and cold.
For sudden the worst turns the best to the brave,
    The black minute's at end,
And the elements' rage, the fiend-voices that
    rave,
        Shall dwindle, shall blend,
Shall change, shall become first a peace out of
    pain,
        Then a light, then thy breast,
O thou soul of my soul! I shall clasp thee again,
    And with God be the rest!

— *Robert Browning*

Terminus

It is time to be old,
To take in sail:-
The god of bounds,
Who sets to seas a shore,
Came to me in his fatal rounds,
And said: 'No more!
No farther shoot
Thy broad ambitious branches, and thy root.
Fancy departs: no more invent;
Contract thy firmament
To compass of a tent.
There's not enough for this and that,
Make thy option which of two;
Economize the failing river,
Not the less revere the Giver,
Leave the many and hold the few.
Timely wise accept the terms,
Soften the fall with wary foot;
A little while
Still plan and smile,
And,—fault of novel germs,—
Mature the unfallen fruit.

Curse, if thou wilt, thy sires,
Bad husbands of their fires,
Who, when they gave thee breath,
Failed to bequeath
The needful sinew stark as once,
The Baresark marrow to thy bones,
But left a legacy of ebbing veins,
Inconstant heat and nerveless reins,—
Amid the Muses, left thee deaf and dumb,
Amid the gladiators, halt and numb.'

As the bird trims her to the gale,
I trim myself to the storm of time,
I man the rudder, reef the sail,
Obey the voice at eve obeyed at prime:
'Lowly faithful, banish fear,
Right onward drive unharmed;
The port, well worth the cruise, is near,
And every wave is charmed.'

— *Ralph Waldo Emerson*

If—

If you can keep your head when all about you
    Are losing theirs and blaming it on you,
If you can trust yourself when all men doubt
    you,
    But make allowance for their doubting too;
If you can wait and not be tired by waiting,
    Or being lied about, don't deal in lies,
Or being hated, don't give way to hating,
    And yet don't look too good, nor talk too
    wise:

If you can dream—and not make dreams your
    master;
    If you can think—and not make thoughts
       your aim;
If you can meet with Triumph and Disaster
    And treat those two impostors just the same;
If you can bear to hear the truth you've spoken
    Twisted by knaves to make a trap for fools,
Or watch the things you gave your life to,
    broken,
    And stoop and build 'em up with worn-out
    tools:

If you can make one heap of all your winnings
    And risk it on one turn of pitch-and-toss,
And lose, and start again at your beginnings
    And never breathe a word about your loss;
If you can force your heart and nerve and sinew
    To serve your turn long after they are gone,
And so hold on when there is nothing in you
    Except the Will which says to them: 'Hold
    on!'

If you can talk with crowds and keep your
    virtue,
    Or walk with Kings—nor lose the common
      touch,
If neither foes nor loving friends can hurt you,
    If all men count with you, but none too
      much;
If you can fill the unforgiving minute
    With sixty seconds' worth of distance run,
Yours is the Earth and everything that's in it,
    And—which is more—you'll be a Man, my
    son!

— *Rudyard Kipling*

from Song of Myself

Who goes there? hankering, gross, mystical,
    nude;
How is it I extract strength from the beef I eat?

What is a man, anyhow? What am I? What are
    you?

All I mark as my own, you shall offset it with
    your own;
Else it were time lost listening to me.

I do not snivel that snivel the world over,
That months are vacuums, and the ground but
    wallow and filth;
That life is a suck and a sell, and nothing
    remains at the end but threadbare crape, and
    tears.

Whimpering and truckling fold with powders for
    invalids—conformity goes to the fourth-
    remov'd;
I wear my hat as I please, indoors or out.

Why should I pray? Why should I venerate and
be ceremonious?

Having pried through the strata, analyzed to a
hair, counsell'd with doctors, and calculated
close,
I find no sweeter fat than sticks to my own
bones.

In all people I see myself—none more, and not
one a barleycorn less;
And the good or bad I say of myself, I say of
them.

And I know I am solid and sound;
To me the converging objects of the universe
perpetually flow;
All are written to me, and I must get what the
writing means.

I know I am deathless;
I know this orbit of mine cannot be swept by the
carpenter's compass;
I know I shall not pass like a child's carlacue cut
with a burnt stick at night.

I know I am august;
I do not trouble my spirit to vindicate itself or be
    understood;
I see that the elementary laws never apologize;
 (I reckon I behave no prouder than the level I
    plant my house by, after all.)

I exist as I am—that is enough;
If no other in the world be aware, I sit content;
And if each and all be aware, I sit content.

One world is aware, and by far the largest to me,
    and that is myself;
And whether I come to my own to-day, or in ten
    thousand or ten million years,
I can cheerfully take it now, or with equal
    cheerfulness I can wait.

My foothold is tenon'd and mortis'd in granite;
I laugh at what you call dissolution;
And I know the amplitude of time.

— *Walt Whitman*

Invictus

Out of the night that covers me,
Black as the Pit from pole to pole,
I thank whatever gods may be
For my unconquerable soul.

In the fell clutch of circumstance
I have not winced nor cried aloud.
Under the bludgeonings of chance
My head is bloody, but unbowed.

Beyond this place of wrath and tears
Looms but the Horror of the shade,
And yet the menace of the years
Finds, and shall find, me unafraid.

It matters not how strait the gate,
How charged with punishments the scroll.
I am the master of my fate:
I am the captain of my soul.

— *William Ernest Henry*

I Am

I am: yet what I am none cares or knows,
My friends forsake me like a memory lost;
I am the self-consumer of my woes,
They rise and vanish in oblivious host,
Like shades in love and death's oblivion lost;
And yet I am! and live with shadows tost

Into the nothingness of scorn and noise,
Into the living sea of waking dreams,
Where there is neither sense of life nor joys,
But the vast shipwreck of my life's esteems;
And e'en the dearest—that I loved the best—
Are strange—nay, rather stranger than the rest.

I long for scenes where man has never trod;
A place where woman never smil'd or wept;
There to abide with my creator, God,
And sleep as I in childhood sweetly slept:
Untroubling and untroubled where I lie;
The grass below—above the vaulted sky.

— *John Clare*

Success

Success is speaking words of praise,
In cheering other people's ways,
In doing just the best you can,
With every task and every plan.
It's silence when your speech would hurt,
Politeness when your neighbour's curt.
It's deafness when the scandal flows,
And sympathy with others' woes.
It's loyalty when duty calls,
It's courage when disaster falls.
It's patience when the hours are long,
It's found in laughter and in song.
It's in the silent time of prayer,
In happiness and in despair.
In all of life and nothing less,
We find the thing we call success.

— *Anonymous*

Lord of My Heart's Elation

Lord of my heart's elation,
Spirit of things unseen,
Be thou my aspiration
Consuming and serene!

Bear up, bear out, bear onward,
This mortal soul alone,
To selfhood or oblivion,
Incredibly thine own,—

As the foamheads are loosened
And blown along the sea,
Or sink and merge forever
In that which bids them be.

I, too, must climb in wonder,
Uplift at thy command,—
Be one with my frail fellows
Beneath the wind's strong hand,

A fleet and shadowy column
Of dust or mountain rain,
To walk the earth a moment
And be dissolved again.

Be thou my exaltation
Or fortitude of mien,
Lord of the world's elation,
Thou breath of things unseen!

— *Bliss Carman*

My Heart's in the Highlands

My heart's in the Highlands, my heart is not here,
My heart's in the Highlands, a-chasing the deer;
Chasing the wild-deer, and following the roe,
My heart's in the Highlands, wherever I go.

Farewell to the Highlands, farewell to the North,
The birth-place of Valour, the country of Worth;
Wherever I wander, wherever I rove,
The hills of the Highlands for ever I love.

Farewell to the mountains, high-cover'd with
    snow,
Farewell to the straths and green vallies below;
Farewell to the forests and wild-hanging woods,
Farewell to the torrents and loud-pouring floods.

My heart's in the Highlands, my heart is not here,
My heart's in the Highlands, a-chasing the deer;
Chasing the wild-deer, and following the roe,
My heart's in the Highlands, wherever I go.

— *Robert Burns*

Letters

Every day brings a ship,
Every ship brings a word;
Well for those who have no fear.
Looking seaward, well assured
That the word the vessel brings
Is the word they wish to hear.

— *Ralph Waldo Emerson*

Farewell, Life

Farewell, life! my senses swim,
And the world is growing dim;
Thronging shadows cloud the light,
Like the advent of the night,—
Colder, colder, colder still,
Upward steals a vapour chill;
Strong the earthly odour grows,—
I smell the mould above the Rose!

Welcome, Life! the spirit strives,
Strength returns and hope revives;
Cloudy fears and shapes forlorn
Fly like shadows of the morn,—
O'er the earth there comes a bloom;
Sunny light for sullen gloom,
Warm perfume for vapours cold,—
I smell the rose above the mould!

— *Thomas Hood*

On Time

Fly envious Time, till thou run out thy race,
Call on the lazy leaden-stepping hours,
Whose speed is but the heavy Plummets pace;
And glut thy self with what thy womb devours,
Which is no more then what is false and vain,
And meerly mortal dross;
So little is our loss,
So little is thy gain.
For when as each thing bad thou hast
    entomb'd,
And last of all, thy greedy self consum'd,
Then long Eternity shall greet our bliss
With an individual kiss;
And Joy shall overtake us as a flood,
When every thing that is sincerely good
And perfectly divine,
With Truth, and Peace, and Love shall ever
    shine
About the supreme Throne
Of him, t'whose happy-making sight alone,
When once our heav'nly-guided soul shall
    clime,

Then all this Earthy grosnes quit,
Attir'd with Stars, we shall for ever sit,
    Triumphing over Death, and Chance, and
        thee O Time.

— *John Milton*

Death Stands Above Me

Death stands above me, whispering low
I know not what into my ear:
Of his strange language all I know
Is, there is not a word of fear.

— *Walter Savage Landor*

Death Be Not Proud

Death be not proud, though some have called thee
Mighty and dreadfull, for, thou art not so,
For, those, whom thou think'st, thou dost
    overthrow,
Die not, poore death, nor yet canst thou kill me.
From rest and sleepe, which but thy pictures bee,
Much pleasure, then from thee, much more must
    flow,
And soonest our best men with thee doe goe,
Rest of their bones, and soules deliverie.
Thou art slave to Fate, Chance, kings, and
    desperate men,
And dost with poyson, warre, and sicknesse
    dwell,
And poppie, or charmes can make us sleepe as
    well,
And better then thy stroake; why swell'st thou
    then;
One short sleepe past, wee wake eternally,
And death shall be no more; death, thou shalt die.

— *John Donne*

The Onward Course

Our course is onward, onward into light:
What though the darkness gathereth amain?
Yet to return or tarry both are vain.
How tarry, when around us is thick night?
Whither return? what flower yet ever might,
In days of gloom and cold and stormy rain,
Enclose itself in its green bud again,
Hiding from wrath of tempest out of sight?

Courage—we travel through a darksome cave;
But still as nearer to the light we draw,
Fresh gales will reach us from the upper air
And wholesome dews of heaven our foreheads
    lave,
The darkness lighten more, till full of awe
We stand in the open sunshine unaware.

— *Richard Chenevix Trench*

POEMS OF COMFORT

Up-hill

Does the road wind up-hill all the way?
    Yes, to the very end.
Will the day's journey take the whole long day?
    From morn to night, my friend.

But is there for the night a resting-place?
    A roof for when the slow dark hours begin.
May not the darkness hide it from my face?
    You cannot miss that inn.

Shall I meet other wayfarers at night?
    Those who have gone before.
Then must I knock, or call when just in sight?
    They will not keep you standing at that door.

Shall I find comfort, travel-sore and weak?
    Of labour you shall find the sum.
Will there be beds for me and all who seek?
    Yea, beds for all who come.

— *Christina Rossetti*

When to the Sessions of Sweet Silent Thought

[Sonnet 30]

When to the sessions of sweet silent thought
I summon up remembrance of things past,
I sigh the lack of many a thing I sought,
And with old woes new wail my dear time's
    waste:
Then can I drown an eye, unused to flow,
For precious friends hid in death's dateless night,
And weep afresh love's long since cancelled woe,
And moan the expense of many a vanished sight:
Then can I grieve at grievances foregone,
And heavily from woe to woe tell o'er
The sad account of fore-bemoanèd moan,
Which I new pay as if not paid before.
But if the while I think on thee, dear friend,
All losses are restored and sorrows end.

— *William Shakespeare*

Friends Far Away

Count not the hours while their silent wings
    Thus waft them in fairy flight;
For feeling, warm from her dearest springs,
    Shall hallow the scene to-night.
And while the magic of joy is here,
    And the colours of life are gay,
Let us think on those that have loved us dear,
    The Friends who are far away.
Few are the hearts that have proved the truth
    Of their early affection's vow;
And let those few, the beloved of youth,
    Be dear in their absence now.
O, vividly in their faithful breast
    Shall the gleam of remembrance play,
Like the lingering light on the crimson west,
    When the sunbeam hath passed away!

Soft be the sleep of their pleasant hours,
    And calm be the seas they roam!
May the way they travel be strewed with flowers,
    Till it bring them in safety home!
And when we whose hearts are o'erflowing thus,
    Ourselves should be doomed to stray,
May some kind orison rise for us,
    When we shall be far away!

— *Horace Twiss*

To Hope

When by my solitary hearth I sit,
When no fair dreams before my 'mind's eye' flit,
   And the bare heath of life presents no bloom;
     Sweet Hope, ethereal balm upon me shed,
     And wave thy silver pinions o'er my head.

Whene'er I wander, at the fall of night,
   Where woven boughs shut out the moon's
     bright ray,
Should sad Despondency my musings fright,
   And frown, to drive fair Cheerfulness away,
     Peep with the moon-beams through the
      leafy roof,
     And keep that fiend Despondence far aloof.

Should Disappointment, parent of Despair,
   Strive for her son to seize my careless heart;
When, like a cloud, he sits upon the air,
   Preparing on his spell-bound prey to dart:
     Chase him away, sweet Hope, with visage
      bright,
     And fright him as the morning frightens
      night!

Whene'er the fate of those I hold most dear
    Tells to my fearful breast a tale of sorrow,
O bright-eyed Hope, my morbid fancy cheer;
    Let me awhile thy sweetest comforts borrow:
        Thy heaven-born radiance around me
            shed,
        And wave thy silver pinions o'er my head!

Should e'er unhappy love my bosom pain,
    From cruel parents, or relentless fair;
O let me think it is not quite in vain
    To sigh out sonnets to the midnight air!
        Sweet Hope, ethereal balm upon me shed,
        And wave thy silver pinions o'er my head!

In the long vista of the years to roll,
    Let me not see our country's honour fade:
O let me see our land retain her soul,
    Her pride, her freedom; and not freedom's
        shade.
        From thy bright eyes unusual brightness
            shed—
        Beneath thy pinions canopy my head!

Let me not see the patriot's high bequest,
    Great Liberty! how great in plain attire!
With the base purple of a court oppress'd,
    Bowing her head, and ready to expire:
        But let me see thee stoop from heaven on
            wings
        That fill the skies with silver glitterings!

And as, in sparkling majesty, a star
    Gilds the bright summit of some gloomy
        cloud;
Brightening the half veil'd face of heaven afar:
    So, when dark thoughts my boding spirit
        shroud,
        Sweet Hope, celestial influence round me
            shed,
        Waving thy silver pinions o'er my head.

— *John Keats*

Life

Life, believe, is not a dream
So dark as sages say;
Oft a little morning rain
Foretells a pleasant day.
Sometimes there are clouds of gloom,
But these are transient all;
If the shower will make the roses bloom,
O why lament its fall?

Rapidly, merrily,
Life's sunny hours flit by,
Gratefully, cheerily,
Enjoy them as they fly!

What though Death at times steps in
And calls our Best away?
What though sorrow seems to win,
O'er hope, a heavy sway?
Yet hope again elastic springs,
Unconquered, though she fell;
Still buoyant are her golden wings,
Still strong to bear us well.

Manfully, fearlessly,
The day of trial bear,
For gloriously, victoriously,
Can courage quell despair!

— *Charlotte Brontë*

The Loom of Time

Man's life is laid in the loom of time
To a pattern he does not see
While the weavers and the shuttles fly
Till the dawn of eternity

Some shuttles are filled with silver threads
And some with threads of gold
While often but the darker threads
Are all that they may hold.

But the weaver watches with
Skilful eye
Each shuttle fly to and fro
And sees the pattern so deftly wrought
As the loom moves sure and slow

God surely planned the pattern
Each thread, the dark and fair
Is chosen by His master skill
And placed in the web with care.

God only knows its beauty
And guides the shuttles which hold
The threads so unattractive
As well as the threads of gold

Not till each loom is silent
And the shuttle cease to fly
Shall God reveal the pattern
And explain the reason why

The dark threads were as needful
In the weaver's skilful hand
As the threads of gold and silver
For the pattern which he planned.

— *Anonymous*

It's Fine Today

Sure, this world is full of trouble—
I ain't said it ain't.
Lord, I've had enough and double
Reason for complaint;
Rain and storm have come to fret me,
Skies are often gray;
Thorns and brambles have beset me
On the road—but say,
Ain't it fine today?

What's the use of always weepin',
Making trouble last?
What's the use of always keepin'
Thinkin' of the past?
Each must have his tribulation—
Water with his wine;
Life, it ain't no celebration,
Trouble?—I've had mine—
But today is fine!

It's today that I am livin',
Not a month ago.
Havin'; losin'; takin'; givin';
As time wills it so.
Yesterday a cloud of sorrow
Fell across the way,
It may rain again tomorrow,
It may rain—but say,
Ain't it fine today?

— *Charles Malloch*

Parted Friends

Friend after friend departs;
    Who hath not lost a friend?
There is no union here of hearts
    That finds not here an end:
Were this frail world our only rest,
Living or dying, none were blest.

Beyond the flight of time,
    Beyond this vale of death,
There surely is some blesséd clime
    Where life is not a breath,
Nor life's affections transient fire,
Whose sparks fly upward to expire.

There is a world above,
    Where parting is unknown;
A whole eternity of love,
    Formed for the good alone;
And faith beholds the dying here
Translated to that happier sphere.

Thus star by star declines,
    Till all are passed away,
As morning high and higher shines,
    To pure and perfect day;
Nor sink those stars in empty night;
They hide themselves in heaven's own light.

— *James Montgomery*

Old Age

The seas are quiet when the winds give o'er;
So calm are we when passions are no more.
For then we know how vain it was to boast
Of fleeting things, so certain to be lost.
Clouds of affection from our younger eyes
Conceal that emptiness which age descries.

The soul's dark cottage, batter'd and decay'd,
Lets in new light through chinks that Time hath
    made:
Stronger by weakness, wiser men become
As they draw near to their eternal home.
Leaving the old, both worlds at once they view
That stand upon the threshold of the new.

— *Edmund Waller*

The Arrow and the Song

I shot an arrow into the air,
It fell to earth, I knew not where;
For, so swiftly it flew, the sight
Could not follow it in its flight.

I breathed a song into the air,
It fell to earth, I knew not where;
For who has sight so keen and strong
That it can follow the flight of song?

Long, long afterward, in an oak
I found the arrow, still unbroke;
And the song, from beginning to end,
I found again in the heart of a friend.

— *Henry Wadsworth Longfellow*

Solitude

Laugh, and the world laughs with you;
    Weep, and you weep alone;
For the sad old earth must borrow its mirth,
    But has trouble enough of its own.
Sing, and the hills will answer;
    Sigh, it is lost on the air;
The echoes bound to a joyful sound,
    But shrink from voicing care.

Rejoice, and men will seek you;
    Grieve, and they turn and go;
They want full measure of all your pleasure,
    But they do not need your woe.
Be glad, and your friends are many;
    Be sad, and you lose them all,—
There are none to decline your nectared wine,
    But alone you must drink life's gall.

Feast, and your halls are crowded;
    Fast, and the world goes by.
Succeed and give, and it helps you live,
    But no man can help you die.
There is room in the halls of pleasure
    For a large and lordly train,
But one by one we must all file on
    Through the narrow aisles of pain.

— *Ella Wheeler Wilcox*

The Day is Done

The day is done, and the darkness
    Falls from the wings of Night,
As a feather is wafted downward
    From an eagle in his flight.

I see the lights of the village
    Gleam through the rain and the mist,
And a feeling of sadness comes o'er me
    That my soul cannot resist:

A feeling of sadness and longing,
    That is not akin to pain,
And resembles sorrow only
    As the mist resembles the rain.

Come, read to me some poem,
    Some simple and heartfelt lay,
That shall soothe this restless feeling,
    And banish the thoughts of day.

Not from the grand old masters,
    Not from the bards sublime,
Whose distant footsteps echo
    Through the corridors of Time.

For, like strains of martial music,
    Their mighty thoughts suggest
Life's endless toil and endeavor;
    And to-night I long for rest.

Read from some humbler poet,
    Whose songs gushed from his heart,
As showers from the clouds of summer,
    Or tears from the eyelids start;

Who, through long days of labor,
    And nights devoid of ease,
Still heard in his soul the music
    Of wonderful melodies.

Such songs have power to quiet
    The restless pulse of care,
And come like the benediction
    That follows after prayer.

Then read from the treasured volume
    The poem of thy choice,
And lend to the rhyme of the poet
    The beauty of thy voice.

And the night shall be filled with music,
    And the cares, that infest the day,
Shall fold their tents, like the Arabs,
    And as silently steal away.

— *Henry Wadsworth Longfellow*

A Good-Night

Close now thine eyes and rest secure;
Thy soul is safe enough, thy body sure;
He that loves thee, He that keeps
And guards thee, never slumbers, never sleeps.
The smiling conscience in a sleeping breast
Has only peace, has only rest;
The music and the mirth of kings
Are all but very discords, when she sings;
Then close thine eyes and rest secure;
No sleep so sweet as thine, no rest so sure.

— *Francis Quarles*

The Rainy Day

The day is cold, and dark, and dreary;
It rains, and the wind is never weary;
The vine still clings to the mouldering wall,
But at every gust the dead leaves fall,
    And the day is dark and dreary.

My life is cold, and dark, and dreary;
It rains, and the wind is never weary;
My thoughts still cling to the mouldering past,
But the hopes of youth fall thick in the blast,
    And the days are dark and dreary.

Be still, sad heart, and cease repining;
Behind the clouds is the sun still shining;
Thy fate is the common fate of all,
Into each life some rain must fall,
    Some days must be dark and dreary.

— *Henry Wadsworth Longfellow*

The Lord is My Shepherd
[Psalm 23]

The Lord is my shepherd; I shall not want.
He maketh me to lie down in green pastures: he
    leadeth me beside the still waters.
He restoreth my soul: he leadeth me in the paths
    of righteousness for his name's sake.
Yea, though I walk through the valley of the
    shadow of death, I will fear no evil: for thou
    art with me; thy rod and thy staff they
    comfort me.
Thou preparest a table before me in the presence
    of mine enemies: thou anointest my head with
    oil; my cup runneth over.
Surely goodness and mercy shall follow me all
    the days of my life: and I will dwell in the
    house of the Lord for ever.

In Beechwood Cemetery

Here the dead sleep—the quiet dead. No sound
Disturbs them ever, and no storm dismays.
Winter mid snow caresses the tired ground,
And the wind roars about the woodland ways.
Springtime and summer and red autumn pass,
With leaf and bloom and pipe of wind and bird,
And the old earth puts forth her tender grass,
By them unfelt, unheeded and unheard.
Our centuries to them are but as strokes
In the dim gamut of some far-off chime.
Unaltering rest their perfect being cloaks—
A thing too vast to hear or feel or see—
Children of Silence and Eternity,
They know no season but the end of time.

— *Archibald Lampman*

Friends Parted by Opinion

As ships, becalmed at eve, that lay
    With canvas drooping, side by side,
Two towers of sail at dawn of day,
    Are scarce long leagues apart descried;

When fell the night, upsprung the breeze,
    And all the darkling hours they plied,
Nor dreamt but each the selfsame seas
    By each was cleaving, side by side:

E'en so—but why the tale reveal
    Of those, whom year by year unchanged,
Brief absence joined anew to feel,
    Astounded, soul from soul estranged?

At dead of night their sails were filled,
    And onward each rejoicing steered—
Ah, neither blame, for neither willed,
    Or wist, what first with dawn appeared!

To veer, how vain! On, onward strain,
    Brave barks! In light, in darkness too,
Through winds and tides one compass guides—
    To that, and your own selves, be true.

But O blithe breeze! and O great seas,
    Though ne'er, that earliest parting past,
On your wide plain they join again,
    Together lead them home at last.

One port, methought, alike they sought,
    One purpose hold where'er they fare;
O bounding breeze, O rushing seas,
    At last, at last, unite them there!

— *Arthur Hugh Clough*

POEMS OF
JOY

My Heart Leaps Up
When I Behold

My heart leaps up when I behold
    A rainbow in the sky:
So was it when my life began,
    So is it now I am a man,
So be it when I shall grow old
    Or let me die!
The Child is father of the Man:
And I could wish my days to be
Bound each to each by natural piety.

— *William Wordsworth*

God's World

O world, I cannot hold thee close enough!
   Thy winds, thy wide grey skies!
   Thy mists, that roll and rise!
Thy woods, this autumn day, that ache and sag
And all but cry with colour! That gaunt crag
To crush! To lift the lean of that black bluff!
World, World, I cannot get thee close enough!

Long have I known a glory in it all,
   But never knew I this;
   Here such a passion is
As stretcheth me apart. Lord, I do fear
Thou'st made the world too beautiful this year;
My soul is all but out of me,—let fall
No burning leaf; prithee, let no bird call.

— *Edna St. Vincent Millay*

A Song

There is ever a song somewhere, my dear;
There is ever a something sings alway:
There's the song of the lark when the skies are
    clear,
And the song of the thrush when the skies are
    gray.
The sunshine showers across the grain,
And the bluebird trills in the orchard tree;
And in and out, when the eaves drip rain,
The swallows are twittering ceaselessly.

There is ever a song somewhere, my dear,
Be the skies above or dark or fair,
There is ever a song that our hearts may hear—
There is ever a song somewhere, my dear
There is ever a song somewhere!

There is ever a song somewhere, my dear,
In the midnight black, or the mid-day blue:
The robin pipes when the sun is here,
And the cricket chirrups the whole night
    through.

The buds may blow, and the fruit may grow,
And the autumn leaves drop crisp and sear;
But whether the sun, or the rain, or the snow,
There is ever a song somewhere, my dear.

There is ever a song somewhere, my dear,
Be the skies above or dark or fair,
There is ever a song that our hearts may hear—
There is ever a song somewhere, my dear—
There is ever a song somewhere!

— *James Whitcomb Riley*

The Dawn

One morn I rose and looked upon the world,
'Have I been blind until this hour?' I said,
On every trembling leaf the sun had spread,
And was like golden tapestry unfurled;
And as the moments passed more light was
    hurled
Upon the drinking earth athirst for light;
And I, beholding all this wondrous sight,
Cried out aloud, 'O God, I love Thy world!'
And since that waking, often I drink deep
The joy of dawn, and peace abides with me;
And though I know that I again shall see
Dark fear with withered hand approach my
    sleep,
More sure am I when lonely night shall flee,
At dawn the sun will bring good cheer to me.

— *Anonymous*

On a Beautiful Day

O unseen Spirit! now a calm divine
    Comes forth from thee, rejoicing earth and air!
Trees, hills, and houses, all distinctly shine.
    And thy great ocean slumbers everywhere.

The mountain ridge against the purple sky
    Stands clear and strong, with darkened rocks
        and dells,
And cloudless brightness opens wide and high
    A home aerial, where thy presence dwells.

The chime of bells remote, the murmuring sea.
    The song of birds in whispering copse and
        wood,
The distant voice of children's thoughtless glee.
    And maiden's song, are all one voice of good.

Amid the leaves' green mass a sunny play
    Of flash and shadow stirs like inward life;
The ship's white sail glides onward far away,
    Unhaunted by a dream of storm or strife.

— *John Sterling*

Laus Deo!

ON HEARING THE BELLS RING ON THE PASSAGE
OF THE CONSTITUTIONAL AMENDMENT
ABOLISHING SLAVERY

It is done!
Clang of bell and roar of gun
Send the tidings up and down.
How the belfries rock and reel!
How the great guns, peal on peal,
Fling the joy from town to town!

Ring, O bells!
Every stroke exulting tells
Of the burial hour of crime.
Loud and long, that all may hear,
Ring for every listening ear
Of Eternity and Time!

Let us kneel:
God's own voice is in that peal,
And this spot is holy ground.
Lord, forgive us! What are we
That our eyes this glory see,
That our ears have heard this sound!

For the Lord
On the whirlwind is abroad;
In the earthquake He has spoken;
He has smitten with His thunder
The iron walls asunder,
And the gates of brass are broken!

Loud and long
Lift the old exulting song;
Sing with Miriam by the sea,
He has cast the mighty down;
Horse and rider sink and drown;
'He hath triumphed gloriously!'

Did we dare,
In our agony of prayer,
Ask for more than He has done?
When was ever His right hand
Over any time or land
Stretched as now beneath the sun?

How they pale,
Ancient myth and song and tale,
In this wonder of our days
When the cruel rod of war
Blossoms white with righteous law,
And the wrath of man is praise!

Blotted out!
All within and all about
Shall a fresher life begin;
Freer breathe the universe
As it rolls its heavy curse
On the dead and buried sin!

It is done!
In the circuit of the sun
Shall the sound thereof go forth.
It shall bid the sad rejoice,
It shall give the dumb a voice,
It shall belt with joy the earth!

Ring and swing,
Bells of joy! On morning's wing
Sound the song of praise abroad!
With a sound of broken chains
Tell the nations that He reigns,
Who alone is Lord and God!

— *John Greenleaf Whittier*

I Hear America Singing

I hear America singing, the varied carols I
    hear;
Those of mechanics—each one singing his as
    it should be blithe and strong;
The carpenter singing his, as he measures his
    plank or beam,
The mason singing his, as he makes ready for
    work, or leaves off work;
The boatman singing what belongs to him in
    his boat—the deckhand singing on the
    steamboat deck;
The shoemaker singing as he sits on his
    bench—the hatter singing as he stands;
The wood-cutter's song, the ploughboy's on
    his way in the morning, or at noon
    intermission, or at sundown,
The delicious singing of the mother—or of the
    young wife at work—or of the girl sewing
    or washing—Each singing what belongs to
    her, and to none else;

The day what belongs to the day—At night
    the party of young fellows, robust, friendly,
Singing, with open mouths their strong
    melodious songs.

— *Walt Whitman*

The Song My Paddle Sings

West wind, blow from your prairie nest,
Blow from the mountains, blow from the west.
The sail is idle, the sailor too;
O wind of the west, we wait for you!
Blow, blow!
I have wooed you so,
But never a favor you bestow.
You rock your cradle the hills between,
But scorn to notice my white lateen.

I stow the sail and unship the mast:
I wooed you long, but my wooing's past;
My paddle will lull you into rest:
O drowsy wind of the drowsy west,
Sleep, sleep!
By your mountains steep,
Or down where the prairie grasses sweep,
Now fold in slumber your laggard wings,
For soft is the song my paddle sings.

August is laughing across the sky,
Laughing while paddle, canoe and I
Drift, drift,
Where the hills uplift
On either side of the current swift.

The river rolls in its rocky bed,
My paddle is plying its way ahead,
Dip, dip,
When the waters flip
In foam as over their breast we slip.

And oh, the river runs swifter now;
The eddies circle about my bow:
Swirl, swirl!
How the ripples curl
In many a dangerous pool awhirl!
And far to forward the rapids roar,
Fretting their margin for evermore;
Dash, dash,
With a mighty crash,
They seethe and boil and bound and splash.

Be strong, O paddle! be brave, canoe!
The reckless waves you must plunge into.
Reel, reel,
On your trembling keel,
But never a fear my craft will feel.

We've raced the rapids; we're far ahead:
The river slips through its silent bed.
Sway, sway,
As the bubbles spray
And fall in tinkling tunes away.

And up on the hills against the sky,
A fir tree rocking its lullaby
Swings, swings,
Its emerald wings,
Swelling the song that my paddle sings.

— *E. Pauline Johnson*

Daffodils

I wander'd lonely as a cloud
    That floats on high o'er vales and hills,
When all at once I saw a crowd,
    A host, of golden daffodils;
Beside the lake, beneath the trees,
Fluttering and dancing in the breeze.

Continuous as the stars that shine
    And twinkle on the Milky Way,
They stretched in never-ending line
    Along the margin of a bay:
Ten thousand saw I at a glance,
Tossing their heads in sprightly dance.

The waves beside them danced, but they
    Out-did the sparkling waves in glee:
A poet could not but be gay,
    In such a jocund company:
I gazed—and gazed—but little thought
What wealth the show to me had brought:

For oft, when on my couch I lie
    In vacant or in pensive mood,
They flash upon that inward eye
    Which is the bliss of solitude;
And then my heart with pleasure fills,
And dances with the daffodils.

— *William Wordsworth*

A Birthday

My heart is like a singing bird
    Whose nest is in a water'd shoot;
My heart is like an apple-tree
    Whose boughs are bent with thick-set fruit;
My heart is like a rainbow shell
    That paddles in a halcyon sea;
My heart is gladder than all these,
    Because my love is come to me.

Raise me a daïs of silk and down;
    Hang it with vair and purple dyes;
Carve it in doves and pomegranates,
    And peacocks with a hundred eyes;
Work it in gold and silver grapes,
    In leaves and silver fleurs-de-lys;
Because the birthday of my life
    Is come, my love is come to me.

— *Christina Rossetti*

Hurrahing in the Harvest

Summer ends now; now, barbarous in beauty, the
    stooks arise
      Around; up above, what wind-walks! what
          lovely behaviour
      Of silk-sack clouds! has wilder, wilful-wavier
Meal-drift moulded ever and melted across
    skies?

I walk, I lift up, I lift up heart, eyes,
      Down all that glory in the heavens to glean
          our Saviour;
      And, eyes, heart, what looks, what lips yet
          gave you a
Rapturous love's greeting of realer, of rounder
    replies?

And the azurous hung hills are his world-
    wielding shoulder
      Majestic—as a stallion stalwart, very-violet-
          sweet!—
These things, these things were here and but the
    beholder

Wanting; which two when they once meet,
The heart rears wings bold and bolder
   And hurls for him, O half hurls earth for him
      off under his feet.

— *Gerard Manley Hopkins*

Over the Wintry Threshold

Over the wintry threshold
    Who comes with joy today,
So frail, yet so enduring,
    To triumph o'er dismay?

Ah, quick her tears are springing,
    And quickly they are dried,
For sorrow walks before her,
    But gladness walks beside.

She comes with gusts of laughter,—
    The music as it rills;
With tenderness and sweetness,
    The wisdom of the hills.

Her hands are strong to comfort,
    Her heart is quick to heed;
She knows the signs of sadness,
    She knows the voice of need;

There is no living creature,
    However poor or small,
But she will know its trouble,
    And hearken to its call.

Oh, well they fare forever,
    By mighty dreams possessed,
Whose hearts have lain a moment
    On that eternal breast.

— *Bliss Carman*

The Year's at the Spring

The year's at the spring,
And day's at the morn;
Morning's at seven;
The hill-side's dew-pearled;
The lark's on the wing;
The snail's on the thorn;
God's in his Heaven—
All's right with the world!

— *Robert Browning*

Cheerfulness Taught by Reason

I think we are too ready with complaint
In this fair world of God's. Had we no hope
Indeed beyond the zenith and the slope
Of yon gray blank of sky, we might grow faint
To muse upon eternity's constraint
Round our aspirant souls; but since the scope
Must widen early, is it well to droop,
For a few days consumed in loss and taint?
O pusillanimous Heart, be comforted
And, like a cheerful traveller, take the road
Singing beside the hedge. What if the bread
Be bitter in thine inn, and thou unshod
To meet the flints? At least it may be said
'Because the way is short, I thank thee, God.'

— *Elizabeth Barrett Browning*

POEMS OF
MOTIVATION

Making Life Worthwhile

Get there from some good
Some little grace; one kindly thought
One aspiration yet unfelt
One bit of courage
For the darkening sky
One gleam of faith
To brave the thickening ills of life
One glimpse of brighter skies
To make this life worthwhile
And heaven a surer heritage.

— *George Eliot*

I Shall Not Pass this Way Again

Through this toilsome world, alas!
Once and only once I pass;
If a kindness I may show,
To a suffering fellow man,
Let me do it while I can.
No delay, for it is plain
I shall not pass this way again.

— *Anonymous*

Self-pity

I never saw a wild thing
sorry for itself.
A small bird will drop frozen dead from a bough
without ever having felt sorry for itself.

— *D. H. Lawrence*

Thinking

If you think you are beaten, you are;
If you think you dare not, you don't.
If you'd like to win, but think you can't
It's almost a cinch you won't.
If you think you'll lose, you're lost,
For out in the world we find
Success begins with a fellow's will;
It's all in the state of mind.
If you think you're outclassed, you are.
You've got to think high to rise.
You've got to be sure of yourself before
You can ever win a prize.
Life's battles don't always go
To the stronger or faster man;
But sooner or later the man who wins
Is the one who thinks he can.

— *Walter D. Wintle*

Time Is

Time is
Too Slow for those who Wait,
Too Swift for those who Fear,
Too Long for those who Grieve,
Too Short for those who Rejoice;
But for those who Love,
Time is not.

— *Henry Van Dyke*

My Triumph

The autumn-time has come;
On woods that dream of bloom,
And over purpling vines,
The low sun fainter shines.

The aster-flower is failing,
The hazel's gold is paling;
Yet overhead more near
The eternal stars appear!

And present gratitude
Insures the future's good,
And for the things I see
I trust the things to be;

That in the paths untrod,
And the long days of God,
My feet shall still be led,
My heart be comforted.

O living friends who love me!
O dear ones gone above me!
Careless of other fame,
I leave to you my name.

Hide it from idle praises,
Save it from evil phrases:
Why, when dear lips that spake it
Are dumb, should strangers wake it?

Let the thick curtain fall;
I better know than all
How little I have gained,
How vast the unattained.

Not by the page word-painted
Let life be banned or sainted:
Deeper than written scroll
The colors of the soul.

Sweeter than any sung
My songs that found no tongue;
Nobler than any fact
My wish that failed of act.

Others shall sing the song,
Others shall right the wrong,—
Finish what I begin,
And all I fail of win.

What matter, I or they?
Mine or another's day,
So the right word be said
And life the sweeter made?

Hail to the coming singers!
Hail to the brave light-bringers!
Forward I reach and share
All that they sing and dare.

The airs of heaven blow o'er me;
A glory shines before me
Of what mankind shall be,—
Pure, generous, brave, and free.

A dream of man and woman
Diviner but still human,
Solving the riddle old,
Shaping the Age of Gold!

The love of God and neighbor;
An equal-handed labor;
The richer life, where beauty
Walks hand in hand with duty.

Ring, bells in unreared steeples,
The joy of unborn peoples!
Sound, trumpets far off blown,
Your triumph is my own!

Parcel and part of all,
I keep the festival,
Fore-reach the good to be,
And share the victory.

I feel the earth move sunward,
I join the great march onward,
And take, by faith, while living,
My freehold of thanksgiving.

— *John Greenleaf Whittier*

Man
from *The Complaint*

How poor, how rich, how abject, how august,
How complicate, how wonderful, is man!
How passing wonder He, who made him such!
Who centred in our make such strange
    extremes!
From diff'rent natures marvellously mixt,
Connexion exquisite of distant worlds!
Distinguish'd link in being's endless chain!
Midway from nothing to the deity!
A beam ethereal, sullied, and absorpt!
Tho' sullied, and dishonour'd, still divine!
Dim miniature of greatness absolute!
An heir of glory! a frail child of dust!
Helpless immortal! insect infinite!
A worm! a god!—I tremble at myself,
And in myself am lost! at home a stranger,
Thought wanders up and down, surpris'd,
    aghast,
And wond'ring at her own: how reason reels!
O what a miracle to man is man,
Triumphantly distress'd! what joy, what dread!

Alternately transported, and alarm'd!
What can preserve my life? or what destroy?
An angel's arm can't snatch me from the grave;
Legions of angels can't confine me there.

— *Edward Young*

Insignificant Existence

There are a number of us creep
Into this world to eat and sleep;
And know no reason why they're born,
But merely to consume the corn,
Devour the cattle, fowl and fish,
And leave behind an empty dish.
The crows and ravens do the same,
Unlucky birds of hateful name;
Ravens or crows might fill their place,
And swallow corn and carcasses.
Then if their tombstone when they die
Be n't taught to flatter and to lie,
There's nothing better will be said
Than that 'They've up and eat all their bread,
Drunk up their drink and gone to bed.'

— *Isaac Watts*

Enid's Song

Turn, Fortune, turn thy wheel, and lower the
    proud;
Turn thy wild wheel thro' sunshine, storm, and
    cloud;
Thy wheel and thee we neither love nor hate.

Turn, Fortune, turn thy wheel with smile or
    frown;
With that wild wheel we go not up or down;
Our hoard is little, but our hearts are great.

Smile and we smile, the lords of many lands;
Frown and we smile, the lords of our own hands;
For man is man and master of his fate.

Turn, turn thy wheel above the staring crowd;
Thy wheel and thou are shadows in the cloud;
Thy wheel and thee we neither love nor hate.

— *Alfred, Lord Tennyson*

Small Beginnings

A traveller through a dusty road strewed acorns
    on the sea;
And one took root, and sprouted up, and grew
    into a tree.
Love sought its shade at evening time, to breathe
    its early vows;
And age was pleased, in heats of noon, to bask
    beneath its boughs;
The dormouse loved its dangling twigs, the birds
    sweet music bore.
It stood a glory in its place, a blessing
    evermore!

A little spring had lost its way amid the grass
    and fern;
A passing stranger scooped a well, where weary
    men might turn;
He walled it in, and hung with care a ladle at the
    brink;
He thought not of the deed he did, but judged
    that toil might drink.

He passed again, and lo! the well, by summers
    never dried,
Had cooled ten thousand parching tongues, and
    saved a life beside.

A dreamer dropp'd a random thought, 'twas old
    and yet 'twas new,
A simple fancy of the brain, but strong in being
    true:
It shone upon a genial mind, and lo! its light
    became
A lamp of life, a beacon ray, a monitory flame,
The thought was small, its issue great; a watch-
    fire on the hill,
It sheds its radiance far adown, and cheers the
    valley still!

A nameless man, amid a crowd that thronged the
    daily mart,
Let fall a word of Hope and Love, unstudied
    from the heart;
A whisper on the tumult thrown,—a transitory
    breath,—
It raised a brother from the dust, it saved a soul
    from death.

O germ! O fount! O word of love! O thought at
    random cast!
Ye were but little at the first, but mighty at the
    last !

— *Charles Mackay*

The Quitter

It ain't the failures he may meet
That keeps a man from winnin',
It's the discouragement complete
That blocks a new beginnin':
You want to quit your habits bad,
And, when the shadows flittin'
Make life seem worthless an' sad.
You want to quit your quittin'!

You want to quit a-layin' down
An' sayin' hope is over,
Because the fields are bare an' brown
Where once we lived in clover.
When jolted from the water cart
It's painful to be hittin'
The earth; but make another start.
Cheer up, an' quit your quittin'!

Although the game seems rather stiff
Don't be a doleful doubter,
There's always one more innin' if
You're not a down-and-outer.

But fortune's pretty sure to flee
From folks content with sittin'
Around an' sayin' life's N. G.
You've got to quit your quittin'.

— *Anonymous*

Procrastination
from *The Complaint*

Be wise today, 'tis madness to defer;
Next day the fatal precedent will plead;
Thus on, till wisdom is pushed out of life:
Procrastination is the thief of time,
Year after year it steals, till all are fled,
And to the mercies of a moment leaves
The vast concerns of an eternal scene.
If not so frequent, would not this be strange?
That 'tis so frequent, this is stranger still.
Of man's miraculous mistakes, this bears
The palm, 'That all men are about to live,'
For ever on the brink of being born:
All pay themselves the compliment to think
They, one day, shall not drivel; and their pride
On this reversion takes up ready praise;
At least, their own; their future selves applauds;
How excellent that life they ne'er will lead?
Time lodged in their own hands is folly's vails;
That lodged in Fate's, to wisdom they consign;
The thing they can't but purpose, they postpone;
'Tis not in folly, not to scorn a fool;

And scarce in human wisdom to do more:
All promise is poor dilatory man,
And that through every stage: when young,
    indeed,
In full content, we sometimes nobly rest,
Unanxious for ourselves; and only wish,
As duteous sons, our fathers were more wise:
At thirty man suspects himself a fool;
Knows it at forty, and reforms his plan;
At fifty chides his infamous delay,
Pushes his prudent purpose to resolve;
In all the magnanimity of thought
Resolves, and re-resolves: then dies the same.

— *Edward Young*

Myself

I have to live with myself and so
I want to be fit for myself to know.
I want to be able as days go by,
always to look myself straight in the eye;
I don't want to stand with the setting sun
and hate myself for the things I have done.
I don't want to keep on a closet shelf
a lot of secrets about myself
and fool myself as I come and go
into thinking no one else will ever know
the kind of person I really am,
I don't want to dress up myself in sham.
I want to go out with my head erect
I want to deserve all men's respect;
but here in the struggle for fame and wealth
I want to be able to like myself.
I don't want to look at myself and know
that I am bluster and bluff and empty show.
I never can hide myself from me;
I see what others may never see;
I know what others may never know,
I never can fool myself and so,

whatever happens I want to be
self respecting and conscience free.

— *Edgar Guest*

Wishing

Do you wish the World were better?
Let me tell you what to do:
Set a watch upon your actions,
Keep them always straight and true.
Rid your mind of selfish motives,
Let your thoughts be clean and high.
You can make a little Eden
Of the sphere you occupy.

Do you wish the World were wiser?
Then suppose you make a start,
By accumulating wisdom
In the scrap book of your heart.
Do not waste one page on folly;
Live to learn and learn to live.
If you want to give men knowledge
You must get it ere you give.

Do you wish the World were happy?
Then remember day by day,
Just to scatter seeds of kindness,
As you pass along the way.

For the pleasures of the many,
May be oft times traced to one.
As the hand that plants an acorn,
Shelters armies from the sun.

— *Ella Wheeler Wilcox*

At Set of Sun

If you sit down at set of sun
And count the acts that you have done,
   And, counting, find
One self-denying deed, one word
That eased the heart of him who heard—
One glance most kind,
That fell like sunshine where it went—
Then you may count that day well spent.

But if, through all the livelong day,
You've cheered no heart, by yea or nay—
   If, through it all
You've nothing done that you can trace
That brought the sunshine to one face—
   No act most small
That helped some soul and nothing cost—
Then count that day as worse than lost.

— *George Eliot*

Work

What are we set on earth for? Say, to toil;
Nor seek to leave thy tending of the vines,
For all the heat o' the day, till it declines,
And Death's mild curfew shall from work assoil.
God did anoint thee with his odorous oil,
To wrestle, not to reign; and He assigns
All thy tears over, like pure crystallines.
For younger fellow-workers of the soil
To wear for amulets. So others shall
Take patience, labour, to their heart and hand,
From thy hand, and thy heart, and thy brave
  cheer,
And God's grace fructify through thee to all.
The least flower, with a brimming cup, may
  stand.
And share its dew-drop with another near.

— *Elizabeth Barrett Browning*

Carpe Diem!

We live not in our moments or our years:
 The present we fling from us like the rind
 Of some sweet future, which we after find
Bitter to taste, or bind *that* in with fears,
And water it beforehand with our tears,—
 Vain tears for that which may never arrive:
 Meanwhile the joy whereby we ought to live,
Neglected, or unheeded, disappears.
Wiser it were to welcome and make ours
 Whate'er of good, though small, the present
  brings,—
Kind greetings, sunshine, song of birds, and
 flowers,
With a child's pure delight in little things;
And of the griefs unborn to rest secure,
Knowing that mercy ever will endure.

— *Richard Chenevix Trench*

POEMS OF
FAITH

Light Shining Out of Darkness

God moves in a mysterious way,
    His wonders to perform;
He plants his footsteps in the sea,
    And rides upon the storm.

Deep in unfathomable mines
    Of never failing skill,
He treasures up his bright designs,
    And works his sovereign will.

Ye fearful saints, fresh courage take,
    The clouds ye so much dread
Are big with mercy, and shall break
    In blessings on your head.

Judge not the Lord by feeble sense,
    But trust him for his grace;
Behind a frowning providence,
    He hides a smiling face.

His purposes will ripen fast,
    Unfolding every hour;
The bud may have a bitter taste,
    But sweet will be the flower.

Blind unbelief is sure to err,
    And scan his work in vain;
God is his own interpreter,
    And he will make it plain.

— *William Cowper*

Pax

All that matters is to be at one with the living God
to be a creature in the house of the God of Life.

Like a cat asleep on a chair
at peace, in peace
and at one with the master of the house, with the
    mistress,
at home, at home in the house of the living,
sleeping on the hearth, and yawning before the
    fire.

Sleeping on the hearth of the living world
yawning at home before the fire of life
feeling the presence of the living God
like a great reassurance
a deep calm in the heart
a presence
as of the master sitting at the board
in his own and greater being,
in the house of life.

— *D. H. Lawrence*

It is a Beauteous Evening, Calm and Free

It is a beauteous evening, calm and free,
The holy time is quiet as a Nun
Breathless with adoration; the broad sun
Is sinking down in its tranquility;
The gentleness of heaven broods o'er the Sea;
Listen! the mighty Being is awake,
And doth with his eternal motion make
A sound like thunder—everlastingly.
Dear child! dear Girl! that walkest with me here,
If thou appear untouched by solemn thought,
Thy nature is not therefore less divine:
Thou liest in Abraham's bosom all the year;
And worshipp'st at the Temple's inner shrine,
God being with thee when we know it not.

— *William Wordsworth*

Hope

Hope is the thing with feathers
That perches in the soul,
And sings the tune without the words,
And never stops at all,

And sweetest in the gale is heard;
And sore must be the storm
That could abash the little bird
That kept so many warm.

I've heard it in the chillest land,
And on the strangest sea;
Yet, never, in extremity,
It asked a crumb of me.

— *Emily Dickinson*

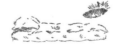

No Coward Soul is Mine

No coward soul is mine,
No trembler in the world's storm-troubled
    sphere:
I see Heaven's glories shine,
And faith shines equal, arming me from fear.

O God within my breast,
Almighty, ever-present Deity!
Life—that in me has rest,
As I—Undying Life—have power in thee!

Vain are the thousand creeds
That move men's hearts: unutterably vain;
Worthless as withered weeds,
Or idlest froth amid the boundless main,

To waken doubt in one
Holding so fast by Thine infinity;
So surely anchored on
The steadfast rock of immortality.

With wide-embracing love
Thy spirit animates eternal years,
Pervades and broods above,
Changes, sustains, dissolves, creates, and rears.

Though Earth and moon were gone,
And suns and universes ceased to be,
And Thou wert left alone,
Every Existence would exist in Thee.

There is not room for Death,
Nor atom that his might could render void:
Thou—Thou art Being and Breath,
And what Thou art may never be destroyed.

— *Emily Brontë*

Spring

Nothing is so beautiful as spring—
    When weeds, in wheels, shoot long and
        lovely and lush;
    Thrush's eggs look little low heavens, and
        thrush
Through the echoing timber does so rinse and
    wring
The ear, it strikes like lightnings to hear him
    sing;
    The glassy peartree leaves and blooms, they
        brush
    The descending blue; that blue is all in a rush
With richness; the racing lambs too have fair
    their fling.

What is all this juice and all this joy?
    A strain of the earth's sweet being in the
        beginning
In Eden garden.—Have, get, before it cloy,
    Before it cloud, Christ, lord, and sour with
        sinning,

Innocent mind and Mayday in girl and boy,
    Most, O maid's child, thy choice and worthy
        the winning.

— *Gerard Manley Hopkins*

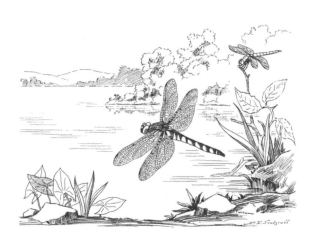

Chartless

I never saw a moor,
I never saw the sea;
Yet know I how the heather looks,
And what a wave must be.

I never spoke with God,
Nor visited in heaven;
Yet certain am I of the spot
As if the chart were given.

— *Emily Dickinson*

On His Blindness

When I consider how my light is spent
Ere half my days in this dark world and wide,
And that one talent which is death to hide
Lodg'd with me useless, though my soul more
    bent
To serve therewith my Maker, and present
My true account, lest he returning chide,
'Doth God exact day-labour, light denied?'
I fondly ask. But Patience, to prevent
That murmur, soon replies: 'God doth not need
Either man's work or his own gifts: who best
Bear his mild yoke, they serve him best. His
    state
Is kingly; thousands at his bidding speed
And post o'er land and ocean without rest:
They also serve who only stand and wait.'

— *John Milton*

None Other Lamb

None other Lamb, none other Name,
None other hope in Heav'n or earth or sea,
None other hiding place from guilt and shame,
None beside Thee!

My faith burns low, my hope burns low;
Only my heart's desire cries out in me
By the deep thunder of its want and woe,
Cries out to Thee.

Lord, Thou art Life, though I be dead;
Love's fire Thou art, however cold I be:
Nor Heav'n have I, nor place to lay my head,
Nor home, but Thee.

— *Christina Rossetti*

God's Grandeur

The world is charged with the grandeur of God.
    It will flame out, like shining from shook foil;
    It gathers to a greatness, like the ooze of oil
Crushed. Why do men then now not reck his
    rod?
Generations have trod, have trod, have trod;
    And all is seared with trade; bleared, smeared
        with toil;
    And wears man's smudge and shares man's
        smell: the soil
Is bare now, nor can foot feel, being shod.
And for all this, nature is never spent;
    There lives the dearest freshness deep down
        things;
And though the last lights off the black West
    went
    Oh, morning, at the brown brink eastward,
        springs—
Because the Holy Ghost over the bent
    World broods with warm breast and with ah!
        bright wings.

— *Gerard Manley Hopkins*

'Tis So Much Joy!
'Tis So Much Joy!

'Tis so much joy! 'Tis so much joy!
If I should fail, what poverty!
And yet, as poor as I,
Have ventured all upon a throw!
Have gained! Yes! Hesitated so—
This side the Victory!

Life is but Life! And Death, but Death!
Bliss is but Bliss, and Breath but Breath!
And if indeed I fail,
At least, to know the worst, is sweet!
Defeat means nothing but Defeat,
No drearier, can befall!

And if I gain! Oh Gun at Sea!
Oh Bells, that in the Steeples be!
At first, repeat it slow!
For Heaven is a different thing,
Conjectured, and waked sudden in—
And might extinguish me!

— *Emily Dickinson*

Blessed Are They that Mourn

Oh, deem not they are blest alone
    Whose lives a peaceful tenor keep;
The Power who pities man, has shown
    A blessing for the eyes that weep.

The light of smiles shall fill again
    The lids that overflow with tears;
And weary hours of woe and pain
    Are promises of happier years.

There is a day of sunny rest
    For every dark and troubled night;
And grief may bide an evening guest,
    But joy shall come with early light.

And thou, who, o'er thy friend's low bier,
    Sheddest the bitter drops like rain,
Hope that a brighter, happier sphere
    Will give him to thy arms again.

Nor let the good man's trust depart,
  Though life its common gifts deny,—
Though with a pierced and broken heart,
  And spurned of men, he goes to die.

For God has marked each sorrowing day
  And numbered every secret tear,
And heaven's long age of bliss shall pay
  For all his children suffer here.

— *William Cullen Bryant*

Life's Lessons

I learn, as the years roll onward
    And leave the past behind,
That much I have counted sorrow
    But proves that the fates are kind;
That many a flower I longed for
    Had a hidden thorn of pain;
And many a rugged by-path
    Led to fields of ripened grain.

The clouds but cover the sunshine,
    They cannot banish the sun;
And the earth shines out the brighter
    When the weary rain is done.
We must stand in the deepest shadow
    To see the clearest light;
And often from wrong's own darkness
    Comes the very strength of right.

The sweetest rest is at even.
    After a wearisome day,
When the heavy burden of labor
    Has been borne from our hearts away;

And those who have never known sorrow
    Cannot know the infinite peace
That falls on the troubled spirit,
    When it sees, at last, release.

We must live through the weary winter
    If we would value the spring;
And the woods must be cold and silent
    Before the robins sing.
The flowers must lie buried in darkness
    Before they can bud and bloom;
And the sweetest and warmest sunshine
    Comes after the storm and gloom.

So the heart from the hardest trial
    Gains the purest joy of all,
And from lips that have tasted sadness,
    The sweetest songs will fall.
For as peace comes after suffering,
    And love is reward for pain,
So, after earth, is heaven—
    And out of our loss the gain.

— *Anonymous*

A Prayer Found in Chester Cathedral

Give me good digestion, Lord,
And also something to digest;
Give me a healthy body, Lord,
With sense to keep it at its best.

Give me a healthy mind, good Lord,
To keep the good and pure in sight;
Which, seeing sin, is not appalled,
But finds a way to set it right.

Give me a mind that is not bored,
That does not whimper, whine or sigh;
Don't let me worry overmuch
About the fussy thing called 'I'.

Give me a sense of humour, Lord,
Give me the grace to see a joke;
To get some happiness from life,
And pass it on to other folk.

— *Anonymous*

Mistakes

God sent us here to make mistakes,
    To strive, to fail, to rebegin,
To taste the tempting fruit of sin,
    And find what bitter food it makes,

To miss the path, to go astray,
    To wander blindly in the night;
But, searching, praying for the light,
    Until at last we find the way.

And looking back along the past,
    We know we needed all the strain
Of fear and doubt and strife and pain
    To make us value peace, at last.

Who fails, finds later triumph sweet;
    Who stumbles once, walks then with care,
And knows the place to cry 'Beware'
    To other unaccustomed feet.

Through strife the slumbering soul awakes,
    We learn on error's troubled route
The truths we could not prize without
    The sorrow of our sad mistakes.

— *Ella Wheeler Wilcox*

The Evening Cloud

A cloud lay cradled near the setting sun,
A gleam of crimson tinged its braided snow;
Long had I watched the glory moving on
O'er the still radiance of the lake below.
Tranquil its spirit seemed, and floated slow!
Even in its very motion there was rest;
While every breath of eve that chanced to blow
Wafted the traveller to the beauteous west.
Emblem, methought, of the departed soul!
To whose white robe the gleam of bliss is given
And by the breath of mercy made to roll
Right onwards to the golden gate of heaven,
Where to the eye of faith its peaceful lies,
And tells to man his glorious destinies.

— *John Wilson*

Anticipation

How beautiful the earth is still,
    To thee—how full of happiness!
How little fraught with real ill,
    Or unreal phantoms of distress!
How spring can bring thee glory, yet,
And summer win thee to forget
    December's sullen time!
Why dost thou hold the treasure fast,
Of youth's delight, when youth is past,
    And thou art near thy prime?—
When those who were thy own compeers,
Equals in fortune and in years,
Have seen their morning melt in tears,
    To clouded, smileless day;
Blest, had they died untried and young,
Before their hearts went wandering wrong,
Poor slaves, subdued by passions strong,
    A weak and helpless prey!

'Because, I hoped while they enjoyed,
And, by fulfilment, hope destroyed:
As children hope, with trustful breast,
I waited bliss, and cherished rest.
A thoughtful spirit taught me, soon,
That we must long till life be done;
That every phase of earthly joy
  Must always fade, and always cloy.

'This I foresaw, and would not chase
 The fleeting treacheries;
But, with firm foot and tranquil face,
Held backward from that tempting race,
Gazed o'er the sands the waves efface,
 To the enduring seas;
There cast my anchor of desire,
 Deep in unknown eternity,
Nor ever let my spirit tire,
 With looking for what is to be.

'It is hope's spell that glorifies,
Like youth, to my maturer eyes,
All Nature's million mysteries,
 The fearful and the fair;
Hope soothes me in the griefs I know,
She lulls my pain for others' woe,
And makes me strong to undergo
What I am born to bear.

'Glad comforter! will I not brave,
Unawed, the darkness of the grave,—
Nay, smile to hear Death's billows rave,
 Sustained, my guide, by thee?
The more unjust seems present fate,

The more my spirit swells elate,
Strong, in thy strength, to anticipate
Rewarding destiny!'

— *Emily Brontë*

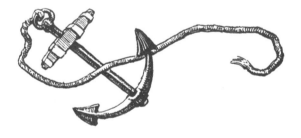

For Forgiveness

Wilt thou forgive that sin, where I begun,
    Which is my sin, though it were done before?
Wilt thou forgive those sins through which I
    run,
        And do run still, though still I do deplore?
            When thou hast done, thou hast not done,
                For I have more.

Wilt thou forgive that sin, by which I won
    Others to sin, and made my sin their door?
Wilt thou forgive that sin which I did not shun
    A year or two, but wallowed in a score?
        When thou hast done, thou hast not done,
            For I have more.

I have a sin of fear that when I've spun
    My last thread, I shall perish on the shore;
But swear by thyself, that at my death thy Son
    Shall shine as he shines now, and heretofore.
        And having done that, thou hast done,—
            I fear no more.

— *John Donne*

POEMS OF REFLECTION

Leisure

What is this life if, full of care,
we have no time to stand and stare?—
No time to stand beneath the boughs,
and stare as long as sheep and cows:

no time to see, when woods we pass,
where squirrels hide their nuts in grass:

no time to see, in broad daylight,
streams full of stars, like skies at night:

no time to turn at Beauty's glance,
and watch her feet, how they can dance:

no time to wait till her mouth can
enrich that smile her eyes began?

A poor life this if, full of care,
we have no time to stand and stare.

— *W. H. Davies*

We Grow Accustomed to the Dark—

We grow accustomed to the Dark—
When light is put away—
As when the Neighbor holds the Lamp
To witness her Goodbye—

A Moment—We uncertain step
For newness of the night—
Then—fit our Vision to the Dark—
And meet the Road—erect—

And so of larger— Darkness—
Those Evenings of the Brain—
When not a Moon disclose a sign—
Or Star—come out—within—

The Bravest—grope a little—
And sometimes hit a Tree
Directly in the Forehead—
But as they learn to see—

Either the Darkness alters—
Or something in the sight
Adjusts itself to Midnight—
And Life steps almost straight.

— *Emily Dickinson*

Change

I shall not wonder more, then,
But I shall know.

Leaves change, and birds, flowers,
And after years are still the same.

The sea's breast heaves in sighs to the moon,
But they are moon and sea forever.

As in other times the trees stand tense and
    lonely,
And spread a hollow moan of other times.

You will be you yourself,
I'll find you more, not else,
For vintage of the woeful years.

The sea breathes, or broods, or loudens,
Is bright or is mist and the end of the world;
And the sea is constant to change.

I shall not wonder more, then,
But I shall know.

— *Raymond Knister*

The Props Assist the House

The Props assist the house
Until the house is built,
And then the props withdraw—
And adequate, erect,
The house supports itself;
Ceasing to recollect
The auger and the carpenter.
Just such a retrospect
Hath the perfected life,
A past of plank and nail,
And slowness,—then the scaffolds drop—
Affirming it a soul.

— *Emily Dickinson*

The Quiet Life

Happy the man whose wish and care
A few paternal acres bound,
Content to breathe his native air
    In his own ground.

Whose herds with milk, whose fields with bread,
Whose flocks supply him with attire;
Whose trees in summer yield him shade,
    In winter fire.

Blest who can unconcern'dly find
Hours, days, and years slide soft away
In health of body, peace of mind,
    Quiet by day,

Sound sleep by night; study and ease
Together mixt, sweet recreation,
And innocence, which most does please
    With meditation.

Thus let me live, unseen, unknown;
Thus unlamented let me die;
Steal from the world, and not a stone
    Tell where I lie.

— *Alexander Pope*

Sympathy

I know what the caged bird feels, alas!
    When the sun is bright on the upland slopes;
    When the wind stirs soft through the
        springing grass,
And the river flows like a stream of glass;
    When the first bird sings and the first bud
        opes,
And the faint perfume from its chalice steals—
I know what the caged bird feels!

I know why the caged bird beats his wing
    Till its blood is red on the cruel bars;
    For he must fly back to his perch and cling
When he fain would be on the bough a-swing;
    And a pain still throbs in the old, old scars
And they pulse again with a keener sting—
I know why he beats his wing!

I know why the caged bird sings, ah me,
    When his wing is bruised and his bosom
        sore,—
    When he beats his bars and he would be free;

It is not a carol of joy or glee,
    But a prayer that he sends from his heart's
       deep core,
But a plea, that upward to Heaven he flings—
I know why the caged bird sings!

— *Paul Laurence Dunbar*

On the Companionship with Nature

Let us be much with Nature; not as they
That labour without seeing, that employ
Her unloved forces, blindly without joy;
Nor those whose hands and crude delights obey
The old brute passion to hunt down and slay;
But rather as children of one common birth,
Discerning in each natural fruit of earth
Kinship and bond with this diviner clay.
Let us be with her wholly at all hours,
With the fond lover's zest, who is content
If his ear hears, and if his eye but sees;
So shall we grow like her in mould and bent,
Our bodies stately as her blessèd trees,
Our thoughts as sweet and sumptuous as her
    flowers.

— *Archibald Lampman*

Dreams

What dreams we have and how they fly
Like rosy clouds across the sky;
    Of wealth, of fame, of sure success,
    Of love that comes to cheer and bless;
And how they wither, how they fade,
    The waning wealth, the jilting jade—
    The fame that for a moment gleams,
    Then flies forever,—dreams, ah—dreams!

O burning doubt and long regret,
O tears with which our eyes are wet,
    Heart-throbs, heart-aches, the glut of pain,
    The somber cloud, the bitter rain,
You were not of those dreams—ah! well,
Your full fruition who can tell?
    Wealth, fame, and love, ah! love that beams
    Upon our souls, all dreams—ah! Dreams.

— *Paul Laurence Dunbar*

Fame
from *Essay on Man*

What's fame?—A fancied life in others' breath,
A thing beyond us, e'en before our death.
Just what you hear, you have, and what's
     unknown
The same (my lord) if Tully's, or your own.
All that we feel of it begins and ends
In the small circle of our foes and friends;
To all beside as much an empty shade
An Eugene living, as a Caesar dead;
Alike or when, or where, they shone or shine,
Or on the Rubicon, or on the Rhine.
A wit's a feather, and a chief's a rod;
An honest man's the noblest work of God.
Fame but from death a villain's name can save,
As Justice tears his body from the grave!
When what to oblivion better were resign'd
Is hung on high to poison half mankind.
All fame is foreign, but of true desert;
Plays round the head, but comes not to the
     heart:

One self-approving hour whole years outweighs
Of stupid starers, and of loud huzzas;
And more true joy Marcellus exiled feels
Than Caesar with a senate at his heels.

— *Alexander Pope*

June

And what is so rare as a day in June?
    Then, if ever, come perfect days;
Then Heaven tries earth if it be in tune,
    And over it softly her warm ear lays;
Whether we look, or whether we listen,
We hear life murmur, or see it glisten;
Every clod feels a stir of might,
    An instinct within it that reaches and towers,
And, groping blindly above it for light,
    Climbs to a soul in grass and flowers;
The flush of life may well be seen
    Thrilling back over hills and valleys;
The cowslip startles in meadows green,
    The buttercup catches the sun in its chalice,
And there's never a leaf nor a blade too mean
    To be some happy creature's palace;
The little bird sits at his door in the sun,
    Atilt like a blossom among the leaves,
And lets his illumined being o'errun
    With the deluge of summer it receives;
His mate feels the eggs beneath her wings,
And the heart in her dumb breast flutters and
    sings;

He sings to the wide world, and she to her
    nest,—
In the nice ear of Nature which song is the best?

Now is the high-tide of the year,
    And whatever of life hath ebbed away
Comes flooding back with a ripply cheer,
    Into every bare inlet and creek and bay;
Now the heart is so full that a drop overfills it,
We are happy now because God wills it;
No matter how barren the past may have been,
'Tis enough for us now that the leaves are green;
We sit in the warm shade and feel right well
How the sap creeps up and the blossoms swell;
We may shut our eyes but we cannot help
    knowing
That skies are clear and grass is growing;
    The breeze comes whispering in our ear,
    That dandelions are blossoming near,
That maize has sprouted, that streams are
    flowing,
That the river is bluer than the sky,
That the robin is plastering his house hard by;
And if the breeze kept the good news back,
For our couriers we should not lack;

We could guess it all by yon heifer's lowing,—
   And hark! How clear bold chanticleer,
   Warmed with the new wine of the year,
Tells all in his lusty crowing!

Joy comes, grief goes, we know not how;
Everything is happy now,
   Everything is upward striving;
'Tis as easy now for the heart to be true
As for grass to be green or skies to be blue,—
   'Tis for the natural way of living:
Who knows whither the clouds have fled?
   In the unscarred heaven they leave not wake,
And the eyes forget the tears they have shed,
   The heart forgets its sorrow and ache;
The soul partakes the season's youth,
   And the sulphurous rifts of passion and woe
Lie deep 'neath a silence pure and smooth,
   Like burnt-out craters healed with snow.

— *James Russell Lowell*

When I Heard the Learn'd Astronomer

When I heard the learn'd astronomer;
When the proofs, the figures, were ranged in
columns before me;
When I was shown the charts and the diagrams,
to add, divide, and measure them;
When I, sitting, heard the astronomer, where he
lectured with much applause in the lecture-
room,
How soon, unaccountable, I became tired and
sick;
Till rising and gliding out, I wander'd off by
myself,
In the mystical moist night-air, and from time to
time,
Look'd up in perfect silence at the stars.

— *Walt Whitman*

Contentment

'Man wants but little here below.'

Little I ask; my wants are few;
    I only wish a hut of stone
(A *very plain* brown stone will do)
    That I may call my own;—
And close at hand is such a one,
In yonder street that fronts the sun.

Plain food is quite enough for me;
    Three courses are as good as ten;—
If Nature can subsist on three,
    Thank Heaven for three. Amen!
I always thought cold victual nice;—
    My *choice* would be vanilla-ice.

I care not much for gold or land;—
    Give me a mortgage here and there,—
Some good bank-stock, some note of hand,
    Or trifling railroad share,—
I only ask that Fortune send
A *little* more than I shall spend.

Honors are silly toys, I know,
    And titles are but empty names;
I would, perhaps, be Plenipo,—
    But only near St. James;
I'm very sure I should not care
To fill our Gubernator's chair.

Jewels are baubles; 'tis a sin
    To care for such unfruitful things;—
One good-sized diamond in a pin,—
    Some, not so large, in rings,—
A ruby, and a pearl, or so,
Will do for me;—I laugh at show.

My dame should dress in cheap attire
    (Good, heavy silks are never dear); —
I own perhaps I might desire
    Some shawls of true Cashmere,—
Some marrowy crapes of China silk,
Like wrinkled skins on scalded milk.

I would not have the horse I drive
    So fast that folks must stop and stare;
An easy gait—two forty-five—
    Suits me; I do not care;—
Perhaps, for just a *single spurt*,
Some seconds less would do no hurt.

Of pictures, I should like to own
    Titians and Raphaels three or four,—
I love so much their style and tone,
    One Turner, and no more
(A landscape,—foreground golden dirt,—
The sunshine painted with a squirt).

Of books but few,—some fifty score
    For daily use, and bound for wear;
The rest upon an upper floor;—
    Some *little* luxury *there*
Of red morocco's gilded gleam
And vellum rich as country cream.

Busts, cameos, gems,—such things as these,
    Which others often show for pride,
I value for their power to please,
    And selfish churls deride;—
One Stradivarius, I confess,
Two Meerschaums, I would fain possess.

Wealth's wasteful tricks I will not learn,
    Nor ape the glittering upstart fool;—
Shall not carved tables serve my turn,
    But *all* must be of buhl?
Give grasping pomp its double share,—
I ask but *one* recumbent chair.

Thus humble let me live and die,
    Nor long for Midas' golden touch;
If Heaven more generous gifts deny,
    I shall not miss them *much*,—
Too grateful for the blessing lent
Of simple tastes and mind content!

— *Oliver Wendell Holmes*

All for the Best

Things mostly happen for the best.
However hard it seems to-day,
When some fond plan has gone astray
Or what you've wished for most is lost
An' you sit countin' up the cost
With eyes half-blind by tears o' grief
While doubt is chokin' out belief,
You'll find when all is understood
That what seemed bad was really good.
Life can't be counted in a day.
The present rain that will not stop
Next autumn means a bumper crop.
We wonder why some things must be—
Care's purpose we can seldom see—
An' yet long afterwards we turn
To view the past, an' then we learn
That what once filled our minds with doubt
Was good for us as it worked out.
I've never known an hour of care
But that I've later come to see
That it has brought some joy to me.
Even the sorrows I have borne,

Leavin' me lonely an' forlorn
An' hurt an' bruised an' sick at heart,
In life's great plan have had a part.
An' though I could not understand
Why I should bow to Death's command,
As time went on I came to know
That it was really better so.
Things mostly happen for the best.
So narrow is our vision here
That we are blinded by a tear
An' stunned by every hurt an' blow
Which comes to-day to strike us low,
An' yet some day we turn an' find
That what seemed cruel once was kind.
Most things, I hold, are wisely planned
If we could only understand.

— *Edgar Guest*

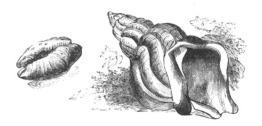

A Bag of Tools

Isn't it strange
That princes and kings,
And clowns that caper
In sawdust rings,
And common people
Like you and me
Are builders for eternity?

Each is given a bag of tools,
A shapeless mass,
A book of rules;
And each must make,
Ere life is flown
A stumbling block
Or a stepping-stone.

— *R. L. Sharpe*

Miracles

Why! who makes much of a miracle?
As to me, I know of nothing else but miracles,
Whether I walk the streets of Manhattan,
Or dart my sight over the roofs of houses toward
    the sky,
Or wade with naked feet along the beach, just in
    the edge of the water,
Or stand under trees in the woods,
Or talk by day with any one I love—or sleep in
    the bed at night with any one I love,
Or sit at table at dinner with my mother,
Or look at strangers opposite me riding in the
    car,
 Or watch honey-bees busy around the hive, of a
    summer forenoon,
Or animals feeding in the fields,
Or birds—or the wonderfulness of insects in the
    air,
Or the wonderfulness of the sun-down—or of
    stars shining so quiet and bright,
Or the exquisite, delicate, thin curve of the new
    moon in spring;

Or whether I go among those I like best, and
    that like me best—mechanics, boatmen,
    farmers,
Or among the savans—or to the soiree—or to the
    opera,
Or stand a long while looking at the movements
    of machinery,
Or behold children at their sports,
Or the admirable sight of the perfect old man, or
    the perfect old woman,
Or the sick in hospitals, or the dead carried to
    burial,
Or my own eyes and figure in the glass;

These, with the rest, one and all, are to me
   miracles,
The whole referring—yet each distinct, and in its
   place.

To me, every hour of the light and dark is a
   miracle,
Every cubic inch of space is a miracle,
Every square yard of the surface of the earth is
   spread with the same,
Every foot of the interior swarms with the
   same;

Every spear of grass—the frames, limbs, organs,
  of men and women, and all that concerns
  them,
All these to me are unspeakably perfect miracles.

To me the sea is a continual miracle;
The fishes that swim—the rocks—the motion of
  the waves—the ships, with men in them,
What stranger miracles are there?

— *Walt Whitman*

Biographical Notes

SIR EDWIN ARNOLD (1834–1904) was born in Gravesend, Kent, the son of a magistrate. Educated at King's College London and Oxford, he worked as a schoolmaster, a journalist and as a senior civil servant. Arnold authored many books, the most popular being the long poem *The Light of Asia* (1879).

MADELINE S. BRIDGES was the *nom de plume* of MARY AINGE DE VERE (1844–1920), a poet who lived in New York City. She published several books of poetry, including *Love Songs and Other Poems* (1870).

ROBERT BRIDGES (1844–1930) was born in Walmer, Kent. He studied at Oxford and became a physician after completing his M.B. at St. Bartholomew's Hospital, London. His first book, *Poems*, was written in 1873. Forty years later, he was made Poet Laureate, a position he held until his death.

CHARLOTTE BRONTË (1816–1855) was born in Thornton, Yorkshire, the third of six children in a family that included the novelists Charlotte and Anne Brontë. With her sisters, she wrote a single volume of verse, *Poems of Currer, Ellis and Acton Bell* (1846). Brontë is best remembered for her novels *Jane Eyre* (1847) and *Villette* (1853).

EMILY BRONTË (1818–1848) was the fifth child born to Patrick Brontë and Maria Branwell in Thornton, Yorkshire. Her sole volume of verse, *Poems of Currer, Ellis and Acton Bell* (1846), was a pseudonymous collection shared with her sisters Charlotte and Anne. Brontë's *Wuthering Heights* (1847), her only novel, is considered one of the greatest works in 19th-century English literature.

ELIZABETH BARRETT BROWNING (1806–1861) was born Elizabeth Barrett Moulton-Barrett in Coixhoe Hall, near Durham, England. Her first book, *The Battle of Marathon*, was published at the age of fourteen. An accomplished and popular poet, she was thought of as a possible successor to William Wordsworth as England's Poet Laureate. She was married to the poet Robert Browning.

ROBERT BROWNING (1812–1889) was born in Camberwell, south London, the son of a clerk with the Bank of England. His education is said to have come primarily through his father's 6,000-volume private library. Browning's first book, *Pauline: A Fragment of a Confession*, was published in 1833. He was married to the poet Elizabeth Barrett Browning.

WILLIAM CULLEN BRYANT (1794–1878) was born in Cummington, Massachusetts. Educated at Williams College, he worked as a lawyer before embarking on a career in journalism. As editor of *The New York Evening Post*, he was a strong advocate against slavery.

ROBERT BURNS (1759–1796) was born in Alloway, Ayrshire, Scotland. The son of a farming couple, his childhood was spent in poverty, with his education coming through his father's tutoring. In 1783, he began composing verse employing the Ayrshire dialect. The publication of his first book, *Poems, Chiefly in the Scottish Dialect*, established Burns as national poet of Scotland.

BLISS CARMAN (1861–1929) was born in Fredericton, New Brunswick. Educated at universities in Canada, Scotland and the United States, he was in his day considered Canada's best-known poet. The first of his many volumes of verse, *A Seamark: A Threnody for Robert Louis Stevenson* was published in 1875.

ALICE CARY (1820–1871) was born on her family's farm in Mount Healthy, Ohio. Shared with her sister, Cary's first book, *Poems of Alice and Phoebe Carey* [sic] was published in 1850. The two poets soon relocated to New York City, where they became popular contributors to a variety of periodicals.

JOHN CLARE (1793–1864) was born in Helpston, Cambridgeshire. The son of a farm labourer, his first poems were written in an attempt to prevent the eviction of his parents from their home. His highly praised first collection of verse, *Poems, Descriptive of Rural Life and Scenery* (1820), earned him the title the 'Northamptonshire Peasant Poet'.

ARTHUR HUGH CLOUGH (1819–1861) was born in Liverpool. At age three, his family immigrated to Charleston, South Carolina. He later returned to England to study at Oxford. Though his first book, *The Bothie of Toper-na-fuosich*, appeared while he was still a young man, most of Clough's writing was published after his death.

WILLIAM COWPER (1731–1800) was born in Berkhamstead, Hertfordshire. He studied at Westminster School with the intention of pursuing a career in law. When the first of many struggles with mental illness put paid to these plans, Cowper found strength in evangelical Christianity. Collaborating with John Newton, he became the foremost composer of 18th-century hymns.

CHRISTOPHER PEARSE CRANCH (1813–1892) was born in the District of Columbia. Educated at Harvard Divinity School, he held a wide range of occupations, including Unitarian minister, magazine editor, caricaturist and landscape painter. The author of books for both children and adults, his poetry was published in one volume, *The Bird and the Bell with Other Poems* (1875).

W. H. DAVIES (1871–1940) was born into a working class family in the Welsh port city of Newport. A poor student, his education came to an end at age fifteen when he began an unhappy apprenticeship to a picture-frame maker. A man who led a very modest lifestyle, Davies' best-known work is *The Autobiography of a Super-Tramp* (1908), an account of six years spent in the United States as a drifter.

EMILY DICKINSON (1832–1886) was born in Amherst, Massachusetts. Though considered one of the great American poets, she published only seven poems – all anonymously – during her lifetime. Introverted and reclusive, Dickinson gained local notoriety for her eccentricities. The first collection of her verse, *Poems*, was published four years after her death.

JOHN DONNE (1572–1631) was born at London. Educated at Oxford and Cambridge, he served as a Member of Parliament. In his later years, he was ordained into the Church of England, eventually serving as Dean in London's St. Paul's Cathedral. Donne's first collection of verse, *Poems*, was published two years after his death.

PAUL LAURENCE DUNBAR (1872–1906) was born to former slaves in Dayton, Ohio. His earliest verse saw print in a high school newspaper printed by his friends Wilbur and Orville Wright. Though he died at a relatively young age, Dunbar produced twelve collections of verse, beginning with *Oak and Ivy* (1892).

GEORGE ELIOT was the pen name of MARY ANN EVANS (1819–1880), born to a farming couple in Nuneaton, Warwickshire. Her education came through boarding schools and access to a vast library belonging to her father's employer. Evans' career in letters began in 1851 as an editor for *The Westminster Review*. In order to ensure that her work be taken seriously, she soon adopted her famous male pseudonym. Though Evans published several works of poetry, she is best remembered for her seven novels, including *Adam Bede* (1859), *Silas Marner* (1861) and *Middlemarch* (1871–72).

RALPH WALDO EMERSON (1803–1882) was born in Boston. After attending Harvard, he worked as an educator, and later became a Unitarian clergyman like his father. In 1832, having determined the ministry 'antiquated', he resigned from the church. An essayist and poet, Emerson derived much of his income through his considerable skill as a public orator. Three collections of poetry, *Poems* (1847), *May-Day and Other Pieces* (1867), and *Selected Poems* (1876), were published during his lifetime.

JAMES W. FOLEY (1874–1939) was born and raised in North Dakota. He settled in Pasadena, eventually working as an editor for the *Los Angeles Tribune*. He published more than a dozen collections of verse, written for both adults and children.

ROBERT FROST (1874–1963) was born in San Francisco. At the age of eleven, following the death of his journalist father, the Frost family moved to Massachusetts. He studied at Harvard and, after an failed attempt at farming, became a teacher. Both critically respected and popular, he served as United States Poet Laureate and was four times a recipient of the Pulitzer Prize.

EDGAR GUEST (1881–1959), known in the United States as the 'People's Poet', was born in Birmingham, England. At age nine, he emigrated to Detroit, Michigan. Guest's first published verse appeared in an 1898 edition of the *Detroit Free Press*, where he worked as a copy boy. Over the next six decades, over 11,000 Guest poems appeared in the newspaper, and in syndication across North America.

WILLIAM ERNEST HENRY (1849–1902) was born in Gloucester, England, the son of a bookseller. Beginning in childhood, he suffered periods of ill-health, which interrupted his schooling. Despite this setback, he had a successful career as an editor for *London* and *The Scots Observer*.

THOMAS HOOD (1799–1845) was born in London, the son of a bookseller. He held editorial positions with *London Magazine*, *The Gem* and *The New Monthly Magazine*, and was part-owner of the literary journal *The Athenaeum*.

GERARD MANLEY HOPKINS (1844–1889) was born in Stratford, Essex, the son of an insurance agent and amateur poet. As a student at Oxford, he converted from Anglicanism to Roman Catholicism and eventually became a Jesuit priest. He worked in the slums of Manchester, Liverpool and Glasgow, and taught Greek at Dublin's Royal University College. It wasn't until nearly three decades after Hopkins' death that the first volume of his verse was published.

HENRY HOWARD (1517–1547) was born to an aristocratic family in Hunsdon, Hertfordshire. He was raised with Henry Fitzroy, the illegitimate son of Henry VIII, a relative by blood. In 1524, upon the death of his grandfather, Howard became the Earl of Surrey. A cousin to Anne Boleyn, Howard was accused – most probably falsely – of planning to usurp the crown, and was beheaded.

WILLIAM DE WITT HYDE (1858–1917) was born in Winchendon, Massachusetts. A graduate of Harvard and Andover Theological Seminary, he authored more than a dozen books and was president of Bowdoin College, Brunswick, Maine.

E. PAULINE JOHNSON (1861–1914) was born on the Six

Nations Indian Reserve in Canada West (Ontario), the daughter of an Englishwoman and a Mohawk chief. A popular poet, she gave readings in Canada, Britain and the United States. Her best-known collection of verse is *Flint and Feather* (1912).

JOHN KEATS (1795–1821) was born in London. An apprentice to an apothecary-surgeon, he published only one volume of verse, *Poems* (1817). Though he died a relative unknown, he came to be recognized as one of the great poets of the English Romantic movement.

JOHN KEBLE (1792–1866) was born in Fairford, Gloucester. The son of an Anglican clergyman, he followed his father by accepting holy orders after studies at Oxford. He later served as Oxford's Chair of Poetry, and is best remembered for *The Christian Year* (1827), a popular series of poems.

RUDYARD KIPLING (1865–1936) was born in Bombay (Mumbai), India and moved to England aged six. Though best remembered for his writing for children, such as *The Jungle Book* (1894) and *Just So Stories* (1902), he produced a wide breadth of work that included short stories, novels, travelogues, collections of verse and an autobiography.

RAYMOND KNISTER (1899–1932) was born at Ruscom in southern Ontario. He attended Victoria College, the University of Toronto and Iowa State University. Though primarily a poet and writer of short stories, the novel *White Narcissus* (1929) was the only volume to be published during his lifetime.

ARCHIBALD LAMPMAN (1861–1899) was born in Morpeth, Canada West (Ontario). His first verse was published while studying at Trinity College, Toronto. Much of Lampman's adult life was spent working with the Post Office in Ottawa. Two volumes of verse, *Among the Millet and Other Poems* (1888) and *Lyrics of Earth* (1895), were published during his lifetime.

WALTER SAVAGE LANDOR (1775–1864) was born into a wealthy family at Ipsley Court, Warwick. He studied briefly at Oxford, but was expelled for having fired a gun in his rooms. A writer of political tracts and essays, his first collection of verse, *Poems*, was published in 1795.

D. H. LAWRENCE (1885–1930) was born in Eastwood, Nottinghamshire. He studied at University College, Nottingham, where he earned a teaching certificate. In 1913, Lawrence published his first volume of verse, *Love Poems and Others*. A key figure in 20th-century literature, he is best remembered for the novel *Lady Chatterley's Lover* (1928), which was a frequent target of censors.

HENRY WADSWORTH LONGFELLOW (1807–1882) was born in Portland, Maine. He was educated at Bowdoin College in Brunswick, where he became a professor. After accepting an appointment at Harvard, he relocated to Cambridge, Massachusetts. The most famous and well-loved American poet of his day, Longfellow's most celebrated works were *Evangeline: A Tale of Acadie* (1847) and *The Song of Hiawatha* (1855).

JAMES RUSSELL LOWELL (1819–1891) was born in

Cambridge, Massachusetts. He studied law at Harvard, but after graduation chose to pursue a life in letters, and served as the first editor of *The Atlantic Monthly*. Lowell's debut collection, *A Fable for Critics*, was published in 1848.

CHARLES MACKAY (1814–1889) was born in Perth, Scotland. After studies that took him to London and Brussels, he embarked on a career in journalism. Mackay's *Extraordinary Popular Delusions and the Madness of Crowds* (1841) continues to be read today.

CHARLES MALLOCH (1877–1938), the 'Lumberman's Poet', was born in Muskegon, Michigan. At age ten, he embarked on a career as a newspaperman by delivering for the *Muskegon Chronicle*. He spent most of his adult life working for the trade publication *American Lumberman*.

EDNA ST. VINCENT MILLAY (1892–1950) was born in Rockland, Maine. She was raised in near poverty, due in part to her father's financial ineptitude. She attended Vassar College thanks to a wealthy patron. After graduation she settled in New York, establishing herself as a poet with the publication of *The Harp-Weaver and Other Poems* (1923), which won a Pulitzer Prize.

JOHN MILTON (1608–1674) was born in London, the son of a composer. Milton attended Cambridge, during which time he wrote some of his finest verse. *Paradise Lost*, his masterpiece, was published in 1667.

JAMES MONTGOMERY (1771–1854) was born in Irvine,

Ayrshire, the son a clergyman. Though a poor student, at a young age he began a successful career working for newspapers. His political writing twice landed him in prison, which in turn led to the publication of his first book *Prison Amusements* (1797). Popular in his day, today Montgomery is best remembered for his hymns, the foremost being 'Angels from the Realms of Glory'.

ALEXANDER POPE (1688–1744) was born in London. A Catholic, he was forbidden by law from attending university. His education came largely through illegal schools. Pope's first published verse appeared in the 1709 anthology *Poetical Miscellanies*. He is remembered today for his translation of Homer and his mock-epic poem *The Rape of the Lock* (1714).

FRANCIS QUARLES (1592–1644) was born in Romford, Essex. He attended Cambridge and studied law at Lincoln's Inn. Quarles held a variety of public positions and, during the English Civil War, wrote pamphlets in support of Charles I.

JAMES WHITCOMB RILEY (1849–1916) was born in Greenfield, Indiana, the son of a wealthy lawyer. Though he left school at an early age, Riley achieved considerable popular success, beginning with his 1883 collection *The Old Swimmi" Hole and 'Leven More Poems*. During his lifetime, he was often referred to as the 'People's Laureate'.

CHRISTINA ROSSETTI (1830–1894) was born into a literary family in London. Her siblings included Dante Gabriel Rossetti, Michael Rossetti and Maria Francesca Rossetti. *Goblin Market and Other Poems*, her first collection of verse, was published in 1862.

MARGARET E. SANGSTER (1838–1912), née Munson, was born in New Rochelle, New York. A prolific and popular writer, she worked as an editor at *Harper's Bazaar*. Her *An Autobiography: From Youth Up* was published in 1909.

HARRIET WINSLOW SEWALL (1819–1889) was born into a Quaker family in Portland, Maine. She began writing poetry at an early age. Her only collection, *Poems* (1889), appeared after her death.

WILLIAM SHAKESPEARE (1556–1616) was born in England at Stratford-on-Avon. An actor, poet and playwright, as the mind behind *Macbeth, Hamlet, Richard III* and at least 35 other plays, he is widely considered the greatest writer in the English language.

JOHN STERLING (1806–1844) was born on the Isle of Bute, off the coast of Scotland. Though he began studies at Cambridge with the intention of entering law, Sterling eventually took holy orders. He published several books in his short life including *Poems* (1839) and *Election, a Poem* (1841).

JOSHUA SYLVESTER (1563–1618) was born in the English county of Kent. He attended King Edward VI School, Southampton, and received a modest royal pension for his poetry.

ALFRED, LORD TENNYSON (1809–1892), the son of a clergyman, was born in Somersby, Lincolnshire. He studied at

Cambridge, during which time his first book, *Poems, Chiefly Lyrical* (1830), was published. In 1850, Tennyson was appointed Poet Laureate, a position he held for over four decades.

HENRY DAVID THOREAU (1817–1862) was born in Concord, Massachusetts. Educated at Harvard, he is best known for the essay *Civil Disobedience* (1849) and *Walden, or Life in the Woods* (1854), his reflection upon simple living.

RICHARD CHENEVIX TRENCH (1807–1886) was born in Dublin. His mother, the writer Melesina Trench, influenced his early literary ambitions. He attended Cambridge and was ordained as an Anglican priest in 1835. That same year, he published his first book, *The Story of Justin Martyr and Other Poems.* A significant figure in Victorian literary and religious life, he served as Dean of Westminster Abbey and Archbishop of Dublin.

HORACE TWISS (1787–1849) was born in Bath, England. In 1811, he became a barrister. A Tory, first elected to the House of Commons in 1820, he is remembered for his creative, if unconventional, oration.

HENRY VAN DYKE (1852–1933) was born in Germantown, Pennsylvania, and was educated in the United States and Germany. A Presbyterian minister, he was the author of popular essays, short stories and poetry. In 1900, he became a professor of English Literature at Princeton.

EDMUND WALLER (1606–1687), scion of a wealthy landowner, was educated at Eton and Cambridge and served as a

Member of Parliament. His first collection of poetry, *Poems*, was published in 1645, two years after he was banished for his support of Charles I.

ISAAC WATTS (1674–1748) was born in Southampton, England. He worked as a tutor and became a prolific writer of hymns. Watts's 'Joy to the World!' has become a popular Christmas carol.

WALT WHITMAN (1819–1892) was born in West Hills, New York, After leaving school he undertook a variety of occupations, including printer, carpenter, teacher and newspaper editor. Whitman's key work, *Leaves of Grass*, first appeared in 1855 as a slim volume of twelve poems. He spent much of the remainder of his life revising the work, adding and, on occasion, removing verse. The last edition, published the year before his death, included nearly 400 poems.

JOHN GREENLEAF WHITTIER (1807–1892) was born in Haverhill, Massachusetts. He had little formal schooling, yet at age 19 began a career in letters. An influential editor, he published several popular works of verse, including the long narrative poem *Snow-Bound* (1866).

ELLA WHEELER WILCOX (1850–1919) was born on a farm at Jonestown, Wisconsin. Prolific and extremely popular in her day, she produced dozens of volumes of poetry. Her first book, *Drops of Water: Poems*, was published in 1872 by the National Temperance Society.

JOHN WILSON (1785–1854) was born into a wealthy family at Paisley, Scotland. He studied at Glasgow University, after which he embarked on a life of leisure. Poor investments prompted careers in law and literature. Many of his most popular writings were written under the pseudonym 'Christopher North'.

WALTER D. WINTLE (dates unknown) is the name credited with the poem 'Thinking', first published in a 1905 edition of *Unity*, the student magazine of the Unity School of Christianity, Unity Village, Missouri.

WILLIAM WORDSWORTH (1770–1850) was born in Cockermouth, England. He completed his studies at Cambridge in 1791, and two years later published his first two volumes of verse, *An Evening Walk* and *Descriptive Sketches*. With his friend, Samuel Taylor Coleridge, he is credited with launching the Romantic movement in English literature. Wordsworth was made Poet Laureate in 1843, a position he held until his death.

SIR HENRY WOTTON (1568–1639) was probably born in the parishes of Bocton or Boughton Malherbe, Kent. He studied at Oxford, during which time he wrote a lost play entitled *Tancredo*. Though his chief interest was science, Wotton was actively involved in the politics of his day. He is known to have written at least 15 poems, first collected in *Reliquiae Wottonianae* (1651).

EDWARD YOUNG (1681–1765), the son of a clergyman, was born in Upham, Hampshire. He attended Winchester College and Oxford. His most enduring work is *The Complaint, or Night Thoughts on Life, Death and Immortality* (1742).

Index of Poets

Index of Titles

Index of Titles

Index of First Lines